PARENT

or

FRIEND?

TRANSITIONING FROM PARENT TO
FRIEND WITH YOUR ADULT CHILD

Mary Ann Froehlich

DISCOVERY HOUSE
PUBLISHERS®

Discovery House is affiliated with RBC Ministries, Grand Rapids, Michigan.

Discovery House books are distributed to the trade exclusively by Barbour Publishing, Inc., Uhrichsville, Ohio.

Interior design by Melissa Elenbaas

Library of Congress Cataloging-in-Publication Data
Froehlich, Mary Ann, 1955-
Parent or friend? : transitioning from parent to friend with your adult child / by Mary Ann Froehlich.
        p. cm.
Includes bibliographical references.
ISBN 978-1-57293-451-1
1. Parent and adult child—Religious aspects—Christianity. 2. Adult children—Family relationships. 3. Intergenerational relations—Religious aspects—Christianity. 4. Parent and adult child. 5. Intergenerational relations.
I. Title. II. Title: Transitioning from parent to friend with your adult child.
BV4529.F75 2011
248.8′450844—dc23

                                                                2011018845

Printed in the United States of America

First printing in 2011

*To my
children and
remarkable
friends,
Janelle,
Natalie, and
Cameron*

CONTENTS

ACKNOWLEDGMENTS

Many thanks to:

My friends at Discovery House, who catch the vision of my projects and expertly bring them to completion.

My husband, John, for his love and tangible support through many years of writing and for helping me to become friends with our adult children.

My children, Janelle, Natalie, and Cameron, who remain the inspiration and teachers for many of my books.

My mother, Maria, for her love, friendship, and enduring example of living life to the fullest and generously sharing it with others.

My dear friends who modeled for me how to become friends with my adult children before I reached that fork in the road.

Contributors who shared their experiences with me: Deborah Casey, Steve Fretwell, Kelsey Fretwell, Miranda Gardner, Isabel Harrison, Pat Haslet, Christy and Scott Henning, Mary Emily and Richard Myers, Janice Orlando, Janae Phillips, Jacquie and Tim Shaw, Donna and Bob Tallman, Christi and Ken Taylor, Leslie Webster, PeggySue Wells, Christine and Kim Williams, Cyndi Wolke, Leann Woolley, and many other parents and adult children who chose to remain anonymous. Some of the family portraits are composites of several similar interviews. Many names have been changed to protect the privacy of families.

We should behave to our friends as we would wish our friends to behave to us.

Aristotle

A friend is one of the nicest things you can have, and one of the best things you can be.

Douglas Pagels

A GARLAND OF GRACE

ATTEND, MY SON, TO YOUR FATHER'S
INSTRUCTION AND DO NOT REJECT THE
TEACHING OF YOUR MOTHER; FOR THEY ARE
A GARLAND OF GRACE ON YOUR HEAD AND A
CHAIN OF HONOUR ROUND YOUR NECK.

PROVERBS 1:8–9 NEB

Julie tells me that her mom is her best friend, the one person she shares everything with in her life. Her mom is the first person Julie calls when she is having a bad day or wants to share good news. They talk often by phone and also enjoy weekly lunch or movie dates. Matt asked his father to be the best man at his wedding, because he considers his dad to be his closest friend. These relationships sound rare but occur more often than we imagine.

What parent would not want to be considered one of their children's closest friends? Yet many adult children dislike or hate their parents. I have several friends who grew up in abusive or negligent homes who would not verbalize that they hate their parents, but they have no contact with them. These friends do not want their children to associate with their grandparents, because they do not respect or trust their parents. No parent sets out to be hated by their children yet it occurs too often.

Friendship between parents and children is not guaranteed. We may not be surprised when adults raised in abusive homes harbor hatred and resentment toward their parents. What puzzles us is when young adults who grew up in loving, healthy, Christian homes have no desire to nurture friendships with their parents. We are equally baffled when we observe wonderful teachers, coaches, pastors, and mentors struggle to get along with their own children.

What foundation did Julie's and Matt's parents build that made their solid friendships possible? When mulling over the topic for this book, I had to ask the most important question. Being close friends with our children sounds ideal, but is it a biblical goal? Does God intend for us to become friends with our adult children? I found the answer to be yes. It is the only way that our children will spiritually mature, placing their trust in God instead of in us.

This is not a book about parenting. If you have adult children, that job is completed. Continuing to micromanage and parent our adult children, communicating the message, "I'm not finished with you yet," has derailed many parent-child relationships. This approach also cripples adult children. The challenges of raising Generation X and Millennials are well-known today, as baby boomer helicopter parents wonder why their adult children often become stalled and enter a period of limbo. The "leave and cleave" Old Testament model—"Therefore shall a man leave his father and his mother, and shall cleave unto his wife" (Genesis 2:24 KJV)—seems antiquated.

This book is about shifting from your parental training role to a new, expanded relationship, based on friendship, influence, and mutual respect. You will always enjoy the unique parent-child *relationship* but the *role* changes. No one takes care of us or cooks for us when we are sick like our moms do, while our dads can fix any problem, no matter how big or small. That irreplaceable relationship remains intact. Yet the role shift is critical to our children's personal and spiritual maturity, as they understand as adults that their heavenly Father is their unchanging, perfect parent. We human parents only pointed the way to Him.

Debbie and Steve tell their children, "We will always be your safety net." This is the reassuring gift they received from their parents, and now they pass it on to their children. My mom says it a different way, "No matter what happens or what crises come, I will always invite you for dinner." Being a safety net is different from rescuing our children from poor choices or letting them take advantage of us, which only cripples them. That does not nurture adult friendship. They must learn firsthand that God's arms are the ultimate safety net.

BIBLICAL SUCCESS

> IT IS YOUR RELATIONSHIP TO GOD WHICH FITS
> YOU TO LIVE ON THE EARTH IN THE RIGHT WAY,
> NOT NECESSARILY THE SUCCESSFUL WAY.
>
> OSWALD CHAMBERS

This is not a book about having visibly successful adult children, using a secular measuring stick. One definition of *success* in Webster's Dictionary is to "turn out well." What parents would not want their children to turn out well? Yet God's biblical definition of "success" is to have an intimate relationship with Him, trust Him with all our heart, and pour out His love in our relationships with others, mirroring Jesus Christ: "Love the Lord your God with all your heart and with all your soul and with all your mind and with all your strength . . . [and] love your neighbor as yourself" (Mark 12:30–31). Following the two greatest commandments is biblical success.

I know young adults who have experienced teen pregnancy, drug or alcohol addiction and recovery, prison time, and other

PARENT OR FRIEND?   12

heartbreaking struggles, yet today cling to Jesus. Without Him, they know they will not survive. They also have close friendships with their parents and families. They are living out biblical success. I also know young adults who are outwardly successful and impressive by secular standards but rarely speak to their parents and communicate less often with God.

LAYING A BIBLICAL FOUNDATION FOR FRIENDSHIP

> I HAVE BEEN REMINDED OF YOUR SINCERE FAITH, WHICH FIRST LIVED IN YOUR GRANDMOTHER LOIS AND IN YOUR MOTHER EUNICE AND, I AM PERSUADED, NOW LIVES IN YOU ALSO.
>
> 2 TIMOTHY 1:5

Paul the apostle did not have children. Instead, he often developed bonds with the younger men he mentored. One of his most well-known relationships was with Timothy. Paul loved Timothy like a son and felt deep affection for him. Yet more significant is the relationship that Timothy had with his mother and grandmother, who laid the foundation for his ministry with Paul. Paul writes to Timothy,

> But as for you, continue in what you have learned and have become convinced of, because you know those from whom you learned it, and how from infancy you have known the holy Scriptures, which are able to make you wise for salvation through faith in Christ Jesus. (2 Timothy 3:14–15)

Proverbs 1:8–9 describes a father's instruction and a mother's teaching as a "garland of grace" and a "chain of honour" (NEB).

Both items represent the gift of wisdom. Timothy wore a garland of grace, given by his mother and grandmother.

A main theme that runs through Proverbs is encouraging adult children to avoid temptation and follow the teaching and example of their parents, staying faithful to God. This is the foundation that Timothy's mother laid for him. Timothy's relationships with his mother and God were built on a foundation that started in infancy and continued into adulthood. The two relationships are linked.

More important than the Ephesians 6:1 mandate that children obey their parents in the Lord and honor their father and mother is the Ephesians 6:4 verse, "Fathers, do not exasperate your children; instead, bring them up in the training and instruction of the Lord." (Other translations state that fathers must not provoke or goad their children.) "In the Lord" and "of the Lord" are the keys to the verses. If our children are going to obey us in the Lord, then they must receive training in the Lord. That's our job. We all know that talk is cheap. The most powerful training tool we have is our example.

We are our children's mirror of Jesus Christ and their heavenly Father. We remember that familiar quote, "You may be the only Bible that somebody reads," and realize this also applies to our children. If we are truly following Jesus Christ and daily practicing the fruit of the Spirit (love, joy, peace, patience, kindness, goodness, faithfulness, gentleness, and self-control), we will earn the love, respect, and trust of our children. This is true for young children, adolescents, and adult children.

Our ability to influence and befriend our adult children is rooted in reflecting Jesus Christ to them. My favorite translation of Ephesians 6:4 clearly sums it up: "And parents, never drive your children to resentment but in bringing them up correct them and guide them as the Lord does" (JB). Adult friendship with our children grows out of love, respect, and trust. Through years of consistent experience, our children learn that they can count on us. We "guide them as the Lord does."

BIBLICAL FRIENDSHIP

Merriam-Webster defines a friend as "one attached to another by affection or esteem." If you are wondering if this is a biblical goal, read 1 Peter 1:22:

> Now that by obedience to the truth you have purified your souls until you feel sincere affection towards your brother Christians, love one another whole-heartedly with all your strength. You have been born anew, not of mortal parentage but of immortal, through the living and enduring word of God. (NEB)

We are born of immortal parentage, beyond our human parentage. Our goal is to feel sincere affection for one another, loving whole-heartedly with all of our strength. Have you ever heard someone make this statement about a family member: "If we weren't related by blood, we wouldn't even be friends"? That relationship is merely tolerated. We want better than that with our children. We want to embrace and enjoy a relationship enhanced by friendship and affection with our adult children.

Paul in Romans 1:9–12 gives us a model of biblical friendship with our adult children or any fellow believer:

> God knows how continually I make mention of you in my prayers, and am always asking that by his will I may, somehow or other, succeed at long last in coming to visit you. For I long to see you; I want to bring you some spiritual gift to make you strong; or rather, I want to be among you to

be myself encouraged by your faith as well as you
by mine. (NEB)

Enjoying a biblical friendship means that:

- We pray continually for our friend.
- We long to see our friend, hoping to visit soon, if it is God's will.
- We want to bring a spiritual gift to make our friend strong.
- We want to be together to mutually encourage one another.

The focus of a biblical friendship is to contribute and give to the other person. The outcome is mutual encouragement. We and our adult children are intended to encourage and support one another.

My favorite picture of an encouraging and loving parent is painted by Donald Miller in *Searching for God Knows What*:

> It makes you feel that as a parent the most impor-
> tant thing you can do is love your kids, hold
> them, and tell them you love them because, until
> we get to heaven, all we can do is hold our palms
> over the wounds. I mean, if a kid doesn't feel he is
> loved, he is going to go looking for it in all kinds
> of ways. Give a kid the feeling of being loved
> early, and they will be better at negotiating that
> other stuff when they get older. They won't fall
> for anything stupid, and they won't feel a kind
> of desperation all the time in their souls. It is no
> coincidence that Jesus talks endlessly about love.
> Free love. Unconditional love.[1]

We hold our "palms over the wounds." We are a garland of grace, passing on wisdom through instruction and our example. We are a reflection of Jesus' unconditional love. We lovingly guide our children "as the Lord does." During challenging days, we may be the only Bible that our grown children read. As our children reach adulthood, we may be completing our daily parental training job but can glimpse a new, extraordinary opportunity to share and impact their lives, perhaps becoming one of their closest, most trusted friends. That is a rare, treasured gift for both of us.

The goal of the following chapters is to help you remove roadblocks to adult friendship with your children and pave the way to encourage it, laying a solid foundation. The lines are fuzzier today about when a child becomes an adult. Eighteen-year-old Kyle joined the military and is serving overseas. He has definitely reached adulthood. Twenty-two-year-old Caroline is a senior in college, which is paid for by her parents. She is in the process of becoming an adult but has not yet arrived because she is financially dependent on her parents. Thirty-year-old Kaitlin recently divorced, lost her job, and moved back in with her parents. Boomerang adult children pose the most difficult challenge to healthy friendship. Just as each of our children is unique, the path to adulthood will be equally unique. There is no formula or timetable. Yet the goal to become genuine friends remains the same.

A few months ago, I arrived at a restaurant early to meet one of my daughters for lunch. Our young female server came to ask me, "Are you waiting for a friend?" I answered, "Yes." After my daughter arrived, our server said in passing, "Oh, I thought you were waiting for a friend. But this is your daughter." I couldn't help responding, "Oh, but we are good friends." I wanted her to know that a child can be the best kind of lifetime friend. This is truly a biblical pursuit.

A GOOD MAN'S FATHER WILL REJOICE AND HE WHO HAS A WISE SON WILL DELIGHT IN HIM. GIVE YOUR FATHER AND YOUR MOTHER CAUSE FOR DELIGHT, LET HER WHO BORE YOU REJOICE.

PROVERBS 23:24–25 NEB

LIKE A SON COMFORTED BY HIS MOTHER WILL I COMFORT YOU.

ISAIAH 66:13 JB

IN THE WILDERNESS, TOO, YOU SAW HIM: HOW YAHWEH CARRIED YOU, AS A MAN CARRIES HIS CHILD, ALL ALONG THE ROAD YOU TRAVELED ON THE WAY TO THIS PLACE.

DEUTERONOMY 1:31 JB

A father shares:

God's Word tells us to honor our father and mother. Exodus 20:12 is the first commandment tied to a promise: "Honor your father and your mother, that your days may be long upon the land which the Lord your God is giving you" (NKJV). We assume that children should respect their parents and treat them well. Yet shouldn't the parents earn that respect? My wife and I believe that we earn that respect from our children by respecting them when they are young. The key lies in the parents' ability to listen to their children. Listening has become a lost art. Having a friendship with one's children requires the art and skill of listening—not acting, fixing, thinking, suggesting, demanding—but coming alongside and simply listening. Children covet to be heard.

My relationship with my adult children has its moments of trials and frustrations. However, my children know that their parents deeply love them. How do they know? They know because we make it a point to regularly tell them that we love them and tangibly express it, with no strings attached.

The other side of showing love is leading by example. A light went on for me years ago when I heard that the best translation of Christ's great commission in Matthew 28:19 is not "Go and make disciples" but rather "While going, make disciples." This is a shared process, experienced with others. As a parent of adult children, I see myself as a mentor, not a manager. My great commission is: While going, mentor disciples. I want my children to pursue their own life path in following God. I am always available to them without expecting them to always be available to me. It is my job to encourage them to achieve their dreams. I made investments for them throughout their lives so that they would not be burdened with debt as adults. I wanted their goals to be attainable and financially possible. Cheering them on to reach their goals has only strengthened the bond between us.

An adult daughter shares:

My mom is my best friend. I have always been able to tell her anything. I can count on her to simply listen and not overreact. My mom is my safe place to be completely honest.

A mother shares:

My husband and I raised two daughters. Our eldest was a superstar. She was focused, driven, and always excelled in school. She attended a prestigious college and law school. Today she has an impressive job as a corporate attorney. Because success came easily to her, she never had to depend on God. In sharp contrast, our youngest daughter had learning disabilities so she struggled in school. She became involved with drugs and alcohol in high school. She didn't attend college. Today she works hard to stay clean and keep a job. She depends on God every day of her life and has an intimate relationship with Jesus Christ. She has a big heart so she participates in a ministry that reaches out to addicts. They listen to her because she understands their struggles. Friends often ask me about my eldest daughter but avoid the subject of my youngest daughter. They don't realize that she is the true success story, the one who God rejoices over.

To welcome mistakes is to encourage learning.

Haim Ginott

Teaching skills takes time, something we often have in short supply. We are often too impatient to let our children make mistakes and suffer the consequences. Our intentions are good, but our behavior actually disables our children, denying them the opportunities to learn adult skills. We instill the belief that we can take care of things better than they can.

Linda Gordon and Susan Shaffer

A resilient mindset, the ability to cope with and overcome adversity, is not a luxury or a blessing possessed by some children but an essential component for all children. Each interaction with our children provides an educational opportunity to help them weave a strong and resilient personal fabric. While the outcome of a specific issue may be important, even more vital are the lessons learned from the process of dealing with each issue or problem. The knowledge gained provides the nutrients from which the seeds of resiliency will develop and flourish.

Robert Brooks and Sam Goldstein

ONE

SOUNDING THE ALARM

CORRECT YOUR SON, AND HE WILL BE A
COMFORT TO YOU AND BRING YOU DELIGHTS
OF EVERY KIND.

PROVERBS 29:17 NEB

You may have noticed that the word *parenting* is not included in the title of this book. In my research for writing this book, I read an abundance of books about "parenting the adult child." It is a familiar topic in our society. The books have chapter titles such as "When Your Adult Child Moves Home," "A Second Chance at Parenting," "Neverending Parenting," "Launching Adult Children," "Forever Parenting," "Interventions with Adult Children," and "Setting Boundaries with Adult Children." It has become an accepted fact that parents will face the dilemma of continuing to raise adult children. Problem solving for adult children has become the new parenting stage.

However, we cannot become friends with our adult children if we are still raising them. Our "verb days" are over. We are always their parents, but we no longer parent them. Our parenting job is finished, though a healthy relationship can endure for a lifetime if we have planted the seeds for friendship.

POST-ADOLESCENCE

Adolescence first became recognized as a stage in human development, from puberty to age nineteen, during the twentieth century. In the twenty-first century, post-adolescence (also called adultescence or adultolescence) is now recognized as a separate developmental stage, roughly between the ages of twenty and thirty-six. Other labels for today's young adults are the delayed generation, start-up adults, emerging adults, and the postponed generation. We parents of post-adolescents have been called helicopter parents, snowplow parents, and perma-parents. It is interesting to note that adolescent and post-adolescent stages were first observed in the middle class, where families were more financially comfortable than lower socioeconomic groups and life was easier for young people.

During the past several years, psychologists, counselors, teachers, parents, researchers, writers, and anyone who cares about young people have been warning us that the current generation of young adults is the most overscheduled, micromanaged, enmeshed, shielded, and dependent generation in our nation's history. What happened to make them this way? Perhaps you read David Elkind's *The Hurried Child* during the 1970s, one of the first books to sound the alarm. Elkind warned that overscheduling and overmanaging children could result in depriving them of a much needed childhood, which would later derail healthy adulthood. Elkind's hypothesis was proved correct. Overscheduling and robbing young people of a relaxed childhood, filled with independent exploration and play, led to them finally pursuing that childhood in their twenties and thirties. Hara Marano says, "The end result of cheating childhood is to extend it forever."[1] (And yet the parenting trend toward overscheduling only intensified and today we seem to have hurried, overmanaged children on steroids.)

In overprotecting children and overmanaging their lives, parents deprived their children of opportunities for problem solving, taking risks, making their own decisions, learning from mistakes (the best teacher), being bored (the best soil for cultivating creativity and innovation), taking charge and leading without adult intervention, and other skills that once were naturally learned as a child. Marano says that many of today's young adults have "experience deficit disorder."[2]

We know that the pendulum always swings in child rearing through the generations. We react in positive and negative ways to how our parents raised us. Our generation's parents were often tough on us, telling us more often what we did wrong than what we did right. We were expected to toe the line with little praise. Our reaction was to become the self-esteem building generation of parents and teachers. We thought the best way to build self-esteem in our children was to protect them from problems, failure, and pain, and daily praise them.

The *New Oxford American Dictionary* defines self-esteem as "confidence in one's worth and abilities." An outgrowth of esteem, efficacy is defined as "the ability to produce an intended result." Efficacy is competence in reaching goals. Our generation didn't realize that esteem and efficacy are built through *not* protecting children from solving their own problems. In *A Nation of Wimps: The High Cost of Invasive Parenting*, Marano summarizes:

> Forget everything you ever learned about self-esteem. Self-efficacy is different. A sense of self-efficacy—a person's perception of her ability to reach a goal—seems to be the critical factor in emotional adjustment. Self-efficacy actually motivates people to take on challenging tasks. The catch is that to acquire a sense of mastery, one has to do things completely on one's own—because the resulting sense of accomplishment is formative and transformative.[3]

To the Rescue

> PARENTS WHO ARE SO ENMESHED WITH THEIR
> CHILDREN THAT THEY FEEL THEIR PAIN AS IF
> IT WERE THEIR OWN MAY ENCOURAGE THEIR
> DEPENDENCE WITHOUT EVEN REALIZING IT.
>
> JANE ADAMS

It is no secret that our generation has struggled with separating from our children. We are the helicopter generation, parental micromanagers regardless of the ages of our adult children. Whether our children are in college, graduate school, or have full-time jobs, we tend to be overinvolved.

We have heard outrageous stories about helicopter parents. I personally know of incidences where:

- Parents called the Resident Advisor at their son's college requesting that he knock on their son's door to make sure he was up for class every morning. The son was not answering their morning wake-up phone calls.
- When they couldn't reach him, parents called Campus Police at their son's university, asking them to check on him and make sure he was alive.
- Parents e-mailed and called each of their son's college professors to check his grades and progress.
- A mother attended all of her daughter's job interviews with her.
- A mother edited her daughter's college applications and essays, and continued to help write her job résumés. If the daughter had a problem with a work project, she would e-mail it to her mother for editing.

College administrators and professors will tell you that they do not have as many problems with their students as they have with their students' parents. Even bosses of young people are shocked when their employees' parents call to complain or try to negotiate their children's compensation packages. The inability to let go is a rampant problem today.

The Millennial generation is the most unemployed and under-employed generation in decades. Young adults have been hit hard by the economic recession. They may have college degrees but are unable to find their first job or, if hired, are the first to be laid off. They are also the first generation to have regularly heard at home, in classrooms, and in the media how special they are just for being them. It's no wonder that one of their labels is the "entitlement generation." Our children are the "special generation," deluged for a lifetime with verbal affirmation and self-esteem–building activities. No resource went untapped to help them reach their potential. Yet they are the least prepared generation for life's strug-gles, expecting mom and dad to come to the rescue. An increasing percentage of college students return home after graduation. Too often mom and dad are more than happy to rescue their children, a situation that cripples their children and prevents friendship between parents and adult children. Healthy, mutual friendships start with weaning children from dependency on their parents.

OVERHANDLED CHILDREN

Diane Worthey is a music educator who has taught children with overinvolved parents for almost three decades. She remem-bers as a child that she loved catching butterflies. She kept one beautiful monarch butterfly in a can and often took him out to play with him. She even took her pet butterfly to school one day. She explains:

> Finally a wise teacher took me aside before I managed to bring my new companion inside the school. She explained to me that by handling the butterfly so much, I had rubbed all of the dust off of the wings, and the butterfly had lost its ability

to fly. This was a crushing blow! All along I had been convinced that this was a special butterfly, one that liked me so much that he wanted to stay by my side. I loved this butterfly and now I had learned that I was the cause of his inability to fly.

As a teacher and a parent, I have often witnessed myself as well as other parents "rubbing the dust" off of children's wings during lessons. With all good intentions, we sometimes hinder and stunt a child's growth.[4]

Well-meaning, loving parents often rub the dust off their children's wings, causing their inability to fly. We overhandle our growing children and then don't know how or when to stop as our children approach adulthood. We misinterpret their remaining by our side as a sign of our special, close relationship.

A Nation of Wimps by Hara Estroff Marano is the most current and powerful book I have read on the topic of helicopter parenting. For all that has been written and discussed for the past three decades about the detrimental impact of micromanaging parents on children, Marano shows that this problem is becoming worse, not better. She explains that today's parents "work hard to clear the path for their kids, push obstacles out of the way, and make the traveling as smooth and safe as possible. They pasteurize parenting."[5] Marano explains that the result is fragile teacup kids:

Helicopters, snowplows . . . the names for pushy parents are proliferating. But they all do the same thing: remove from their children opportunities for learning how to problem-solve. And so far there seems to be only one name for the children—teacup kids. Because, as we will see, without opportunities to experience themselves, to develop and call on their own inner resources, to test their own limits, to develop confidence in themselves as problem solvers, they are fragile and shatter easily.[6]

When we see that our children are unprepared for navigating life, we should respond by gradually letting go to allow them to learn as they mature. Snowplow parents take the opposite tack; they respond by continuing to navigate life for children on university campuses and in the workplace. They are so wrapped up in their children's lives that they don't want to separate from them. They embrace the cell phone as a tool to be in constant contact. Our parents didn't have this option. Marano calls cell phone use the eternal umbilical cord.[7] After reading Marano's book, I realized the highest, saddest price for enmeshed parents who can't separate from their children will be losing what they most desire. They will never enjoy adult friendship with their children.

CHRIST TRANSCENDS CULTURE

> FAITH IS NOT TAUGHT BUT CAUGHT ALONG THE WAY.
>
> MARK SCHULTZ

In contrast to the sounding alarms in our culture, I know many young people who are mature, independent, self-sufficient adults. They hit the ground running and never entered the limbo of post-adolescence. They are caring people who love God and are committed to following Jesus Christ. They are not self-consumed but reach out to help others in need. They are responsible and know how to work hard. They can solve problems and persevere through obstacles. They set significant goals and reach them. They evidence self-respect, self-esteem, and self-efficacy. They also enjoy great friendships with their parents and siblings. They definitely do not act like the postponed generation.

Knowing these young people inspired me to pursue this book project. Dennis Guernsey, one of my favorite seminary professors, said decades ago, "We need to study what families are doing right, instead of focusing on what they are doing wrong." I began interviewing adults of all ages about their parent/child friendships. I especially enjoyed talking to young adults. When I interviewed parents, I tried to verify as often as possible that their perceptions of their parenting methods were shared by their adult children. Their views were often identical. You are reading parts of these interviews between chapters.

Above the clamor of sounding alarms, here is truth we can cling to: *Following the living Christ always transcends culture and society.* When we follow biblical truth and principles, mirror Jesus Christ in our relationships, and trust God with our whole hearts, we hold the key to navigating our culture's challenges. As believers, we will stand out as taking a different path. Through many years of reading and writing about family relationships, I have learned that when a new guideline for healthy relationships is espoused, God usually said it first. He knows how we best relate to one another because He created us. As our heavenly Father, He understands us better than any human being can.

In the next chapter, we will look at the crucial model Jesus gives us for guiding our adult children. Then in chapter 3, we will look at the common parenting characteristics of families that nurtured strong adult friendships between parents and children. There are two parts to becoming adult friends with our children. Friendship is one part. The second part is that we must first both be separate, independent adults.

IN PART WE'RE CREATING A NATION OF WIMPS BECAUSE PARENTS WANT THEIR CHILDREN TO BE HAPPY, AND THEY WANT TO BE THE ONES WHO MAKE THEIR CHILDREN HAPPY. IF THEIR CHILD IS UNHAPPY EVEN BRIEFLY, THEY TAKE IT AS A

SIGN THEY'RE NOT DOING A GOOD JOB PARENT-ING. IN THIS CONFUSED CLIMATE, THEY COME TO BELIEVE THAT ONE WAY TO MAKE THEIR KIDS HAPPY IS TO MAKE THINGS EASY FOR THEM, SO THEY DON'T HAVE TO STRUGGLE OR SUFFER. CHILDREN'S HAPPINESS AND EMOTIONAL FUL-FILLMENT HAVE SUPERSEDED INDEPENDENCE AS THE PRIMARY GOAL OF PARENTING.

HARA MARANO

I LEARNED LONG AGO THAT GOD'S PURPOSE IN REDEEMING US IS NOT TO PRIMARILY MAKE OUR LIVES HAPPY, HEALTHY, OR FREE FROM TROU-BLE. GOD'S PURPOSE IN REDEEMING US IS TO MAKE US MORE LIKE JESUS.

JONI EARECKSON TADA

An adult daughter shares:

My mom has always been my best friend. I was the youngest child in our family. My siblings never experienced that close friendship with her. Because Mom was more relaxed when I was young, she took the time to play with me. We often had spontaneous afternoon tea parties. We enjoyed spending time together, which never changed as I became an adult. My mom found the perfect balance in nurturing our friendship. Though we were quite close, she never held me back or made me feel guilty when I left home during high school to work during summers, attended college out of state, or moved across the country to settle down with my husband. Her visits have been highlights in my life. I love visiting her because she pampers me and I can completely relax. Her gift to me is that she is genuinely interested in my life, without being intrusive or judgmental. She asks questions and converses with me as best friends do.

An adult son shares:

I have one older sister and two younger sisters. While growing up, I often wanted a brother, but as an adult, I realize that my dad and I shared a special bond. I am a reserved person like my dad. Living in a household of four talkative females, my dad would sometimes tell me, "Let's go have some men time," and take me fishing, golfing, to the baseball field to play catch, or out to the garage to work on a project. I have always been close to my mom and sisters but my dad wisely understood that I needed time alone with him. Men do not usually plan time for deep discussions. Topics just naturally come up while we are engaged in other activities. As I became older, this is how my dad talked with me about serious subjects and my faith. Today we still fish, golf, and attend ball games together. My dad is one of my closest friends.

An adult son shares:

I'm the middle child in our family's birth order. My siblings and I are now adults. My parents overmanaged my older sister and over-protected my younger brother, who still lives at home. My parents never micromanaged me, and they allowed me to be more inde-pendent than my siblings. I enjoy spending time with my parents. I can tell them anything and they do not judge me. Though my par-ents appear to be more involved with my siblings, the truth is that I have the best relationship with them. We are good friends because they treat me like an adult.

An adult daughter shares:

My parents and I are good friends today because I grew up respecting them. They were consistent on all issues, unwavering in their faith. I always knew where they stood, even when I disagreed with them. I still trust them to be my anchor.

The father-son relationship is perhaps the most important discipleship opportunity in the life of a young man. As a father walks with God and invites his son into that journey, the son has the best chance to experience for himself the essence of a vibrant, alive faith.

Chap Clark

Friendship is a sheltering tree.

Samuel Taylor Coleridge

Change is inevitable. A daughter will become a woman. As she begins to think for herself, to assert herself, a father's role changes. He can be a friend, an ally, and a trusted confidant if he recognizes that change will come. The father who carefully plants, lovingly waters, and mercifully prunes—and who places his ultimate trust in his heavenly Father—will someday be close to his daughter. The roots of connection will be deeply embedded in the soil of the trust and intimacy he has built with her.

Chap and Dee Clark

TWO

FOLLOWING JESUS CHRIST, OUR MODEL

AT THAT TIME JESUS, FULL OF JOY THROUGH THE HOLY SPIRIT, SAID, "I PRAISE YOU, FATHER, LORD OF HEAVEN AND EARTH, BECAUSE YOU HAVE HIDDEN THESE THINGS FROM THE WISE AND LEARNED, AND REVEALED THEM TO LITTLE CHILDREN. YES, FATHER, FOR THIS WAS YOUR GOOD PLEASURE."

LUKE 10:21

First and foremost, we are followers of Jesus Christ. We continually reread the Gospels to come face-to-face with the living Christ, our Father God incarnate. We want to hear Jesus' words and see Him in action. We view all of Scripture through the lens of the Gospels. At first glance, we might think that Jesus has little to teach us about relating to our adult children. He did not marry nor raise children. Since Jesus was never a parent, He cannot provide us with a model for parenting adult children. Or can He?

Jesus' disciples were a diverse group with varied backgrounds. Yet many scholars think that the majority of disciples were in their mid-teen years. Perhaps some of the disciples were around eighteen years old when they were dealing with the crucifixion of

Jesus. They were young adult men, "people in process." This is why Jesus chose them. They were moldable and open to influence. Even established Saul, who was determined to destroy the church, was a young man (Acts 7:58).

I credit my oldest daughter with inspiring me to research this idea. On spring break trips home, she and her seminary friends have always shared with me what they were learning in class. During one break, my daughter told me, "Mom, next time you read the Gospels, imagine the disciples around our age. It will revolutionize your view of them." She was right. I too had learned in seminary, thirty years ago, that the disciples were young men. Yet at the time, I was not as impressed as I am today. I now view these young adults as a parent would. I relate to Jesus' unconditional love and endless patience for his disciples as well as His complete exasperation at times.

Scripture does not tell us the exact ages of the twelve disciples and we can only speculate. Men under twenty were not required to pay Roman taxes, which leads some scholars to believe that all disciples were under twenty, except Peter and Matthew. Matthew was a tax collector. Peter was the only disciple we know to be married (Matthew 8:14), and he was probably in his early twenties. The rest were likely minimally educated, having become apprentices to their fathers at the age of fifteen. (In the disciples' culture, it was normal for a fifteen-year-old young man to either become a disciple to a rabbi or apprentice with his father in his trade.) In contrast, Jesus began His ministry after He turned thirty, the legal age required to be consecrated to enter the priesthood.

We may not know the exact ages of the disciples, but what we do know is that Jesus was their mentor, teacher, caretaker, mediator, and guide. He passionately loved them. Jesus acted as their parent, their perfect, heavenly parent. The disciples quickly believed in Jesus and left everything to follow Him (Mark 10:28). In contrast to Paul, the disciples didn't have a lot to lose. When Jesus asked them to come spend the day with Him, we can almost see the first disciples shrug their shoulders and reply, "Sure, why not?" (see John 1:37–43). In contrast to the established religious leaders who were angered and threatened by Jesus' claims, the disciples rarely questioned Jesus or argued with Him. They were completely trusting.

"ARE YOU SO DULL?"

Because the disciples were raised in a radically different culture than our own, we cannot make the mistake of imagining them as American teenagers or young adults. Yet some of the disciples' behaviors do sound familiar to us even in the twenty-first century.

Throughout the Gospels, the disciples are concerned with food and when they are going to eat. No matter how many times Jesus provides them with plenty to eat, they continue to worry about their next meal. They often fall asleep at the worst possible times (the Transfiguration and Garden of Gethsemane). They are forgetful. They are impulsive and reactive. They are easily irritated by young children. They are self-consumed. They are jealous and argue about which one of them is the best and most important disciple to Jesus. (Remember that Jesus has two sets of brothers in his group.) Jesus must often remind His disciples to be discreet and not share too much information with the crowds—a challenge for any young person. The disciples experience a roller-coaster of emotions—fear, astonishment, amazement, surprise, and terror—in short periods of time, and are quick to act on these emotions. Within hours of pledging their undying devotion to Jesus, they become frightened and run away.

No matter how many ways or how often Jesus explains His mission on earth, the disciples are usually confused. They listen to Jesus instruct the crowds with parables, but the disciples don't understand the stories. In Mark 4, when the disciples ask Jesus to explain the parable of the sower, He answers, "Don't you understand this parable? How then will you understand any parable?"

(v. 13). In Mark 7, the disciples don't understand another parable and a clearly frustrated Jesus responds, "Are you so dull?" (v. 18). *Are you so dense, so dumb?* Jesus tries a different approach: "With many similar parables Jesus spoke the word to them [the crowds], as much as they could understand. He did not say anything to them without using a parable. But when he was alone with his own disciples, he explained everything" (Mark 4:33–34).

As parents, we can relate to what Jesus must have felt when He listened to Peter impulsively declare, "Even if all fall away, I will not. Even if I have to die with you, I will never disown you" (Mark 14:29, 31). Peter's words did not match his behavior. Soon Peter, James, and John are sound asleep in the Garden of Gethsemane. Wrestling with deep despair and sorrow, Jesus tries to wake them three times to have them watch and pray. The third time he says to them, "Are you still sleeping and resting? Enough! The hour has come" (v. 41). After Judas identifies Jesus to the crowd as the man to arrest, Peter cuts off the high priest's servant's ear, forcing Jesus to parent again ("No more of this!"). Then the terrified disciples scatter and desert Jesus. Peter disowns His Lord three times and weeps bitterly afterward.

"DON'T YOU REMEMBER?"

This incident is my personal favorite. It's easy to imagine our own adult children (not at their best) as part of this disciples' group. Jesus had fed five thousand people with five loaves and two fish on an earlier occasion (Mark 6:37–44). The disciples had initially wanted to send the people away to buy their own food (Mark 6:36), but Jesus was teaching the disciples to provide nourishment for the crowd. Jesus is the ultimate host and provider. Throughout the Gospels, He consistently has compassion for hungry, exhausted, weak, and broken human beings. Jesus is "filled with compassion" when he heals the sick, feeds the hungry, and comforts hurting people. Jesus understands basic human needs. His compassion is always backed up by action. This is what He was trying to teach

His disciples. When Jesus explains that He is the Bread of Life, He is communicating tangible truth to His followers.

You would think that such a remarkable miracle as feeding five thousand people would be hard to forget. Yet in Mark chapter 8, Jesus seems to be starting from scratch with the disciples:

> During those days another large crowd gathered. Since they had nothing to eat, Jesus called his disciples to him and said, "I have compassion for these people; they have already been with me three days and have nothing to eat. If I send them home hungry, they will collapse on the way, because some of them have come a long distance." His disciples answered, "But where in this remote place can anyone get enough bread to feed them?" (vv. 1–4)

They really can't remember? Jesus then calmly asks the disciples, "How many loaves do you have?" (v. 5) and feeds four thousand people with seven loaves of bread and a few fish. And when they get back in the boat, the disciples have forgotten to bring bread! They had one loaf left in the boat.

Jesus tries to teach using this experience and warns them, "Watch out for the yeast of the Pharisees and that of Herod" (v. 15). They discuss this with each other and say, "It is because we have no bread" (v. 16). These young men are concrete, literal thinkers, unable to make any connections beyond their own experience. Jesus speaks more directly to them:

> "Why are you talking about having no bread? Do you still not see or understand? Are your hearts hardened? Do you have eyes but fail to see, and ears but fail to hear? And don't you remember? When I broke the five loaves for the five thousand, how many basketfuls of pieces did you pick up?"

"Twelve," they replied.

"And when I broke the seven loaves for the four thousand, how many basketfuls of pieces did you pick up?"

They answered, "Seven."

He said to them, "Do you still not understand?" (Mark 8:17–21)

As parents, we relate to Jesus' disbelief, disappointment, and frustration with His adult children. We also relate to His continuing patience and unconditional love for them. Now let's observe the ways that Jesus consistently nurtures His young adult children.

JESUS NURTURES THE DISCIPLES

Jesus makes time for the disciples. Jesus' ministry was more stressful and consuming than any corporate job. The crowds constantly followed Jesus, making increasing demands on His time. Throughout the Gospels, Jesus regularly takes the disciples away to recover and spend intimate time alone with Him. Mark 9:30–31 says, "Jesus did not want anyone to know where they were, because he was teaching his disciples." Early in His ministry, we find Jesus just hanging out for the day with some of His disciples (John 1:39, 3:22). He does not have an appointment, a schedule, or an agenda set with these young men. He builds deep relationships with them through spending unstructured time together. There is no substitute.

> THEY SAID, "RABBI" (WHICH MEANS TEACHER), "WHERE ARE YOU STAYING?" "COME," HE REPLIED, "AND YOU WILL SEE." SO THEY WENT AND SAW WHERE HE WAS STAYING, AND SPENT THAT DAY WITH HIM.
>
> JOHN 1:38–39

Jesus understands and provides for the disciples' physical needs. Jesus consistently has compassion for the disciples' as well as the crowd's basic human needs. He is the disciples' caretaker, providing meals for them as well as making sure they are rested. No wonder Jesus specifically tells the disciples not to worry about what they will eat or wear (Luke 12:22). Jesus knows how weak His children are, only made worse by hunger or exhaustion. Mark 6:30–32 reads, "The apostles gathered around Jesus and reported to him all they had done and taught. Then, because so many people were coming and going that they did not even have a chance to eat, he said to them, 'Come with me by yourselves to a quiet place and get some rest.' So they went away by themselves in a boat to a solitary place." After the disciples report to Jesus, He provides them with recovery time.

As Jesus took care of His disciples, the women took care of the needs of Jesus (Matthew 27:55). These women were also followers and a few were mothers of disciples (Matthew 27:56). Jesus' female followers contributed financially "out of their own means" to support Jesus and His disciples (Luke 8:2–3). The women stayed faithful to Jesus through His crucifixion. With the exception of John, all the other disciples scattered. When we understand the devotion of these motherly followers to Jesus, we are not surprised that He first appears to Mary Magdalene (Mark 16:9).

Jesus may become exasperated with His disciples but He is never angry. We see Jesus become frustrated with the disciples. We observe His disappointment at times. But He never becomes angry with them. Jesus does become angry, downright furious at times, with the Pharisees and religious establishment (Mark 3:5, 11:15). Yet with His disciples, Jesus is infinitely patient with their lack of understanding. He is their guide and teacher, responsible for their growth.

Jesus does become angry with Peter when Peter rebukes Jesus about His mission (Mark 8:32–33). Jesus seems to be consistently tougher on Peter than the other disciples. He is preparing him for leadership.

Jesus is a guide, not an authoritarian parent figure. If there is any parent who should be able to say, "You will do it because I said so," that would be God incarnate. Yet Jesus rarely lectures the disciples or is dictatorial with them. Instead He asks them questions, listens to them, encourages them to talk to Him, tells them stories, and repeatedly explains concepts in various ways that they can grasp. No matter how "dull" the disciples are, He never gives up on them. As the disciples slowly mature, Jesus shares more information with them.

Jesus is open and honest with the disciples, preparing them for the future. Jesus knows that His days on earth are coming to an end. When His closest disciples ask Him what the future will bring, He is honest with them. In Mark chapter 13, He tells them the truth in detail, preparing them and warning them about the future. In Mark 14:18, Jesus tells His disciples, "I tell you the truth, one of you will betray me—one who is eating with me." The time for telling parables and stories is now past.

> "DO YOU SEE ALL THESE GREAT BUILDINGS?" REPLIED JESUS. "NOT ONE STONE HERE WILL BE LEFT ON ANOTHER; EVERY ONE WILL BE THROWN DOWN." AS JESUS WAS SITTING ON THE MOUNT OF OLIVES OPPOSITE THE TEMPLE, PETER, JAMES, JOHN AND ANDREW ASKED HIM PRIVATELY, "TELL US, WHEN WILL THESE THINGS HAPPEN? AND WHAT WILL BE THE SIGN THAT THEY ARE ALL ABOUT TO BE FULFILLED?"
>
> MARK 13:2–4

Jesus defends His disciples when the religious establishment criticizes them. Jesus knows the hearts of His disciples and will not tolerate criticism for irrelevant external behaviors. When the Pharisees criticize the disciples for eating with unwashed hands, Jesus answers, "You have a fine way of setting aside the commands of

God in order to observe your own traditions!" (Mark 7:9). When the Pharisees criticize the disciples for eating, drinking, or working on the Sabbath, instead of fasting and praying (Luke 5:33, 6:1–2), Jesus responds:

> Have you never read what David did when he and his companions were hungry? He entered the house of God, and taking the consecrated bread, he ate what is lawful only for priests to eat. And he also gave some to his companions . . . The Son of Man is Lord of the Sabbath. (Luke 6:3–5)

Jesus enjoys intimacy with His "favorite disciples" and makes them feel special to Him. Jesus has a special bond with the two sets of brothers whom He first called to follow Him, Peter and Andrew, James and John. They are His inner circle. He confides in them, asks them to accompany Him on special occasions, and enjoys spending time with them. They know how special they are to Him. Jesus cultivates deep, individual relationships. According to John, he is Jesus' favorite, beloved disciple. John is the only disciple who joins the women to witness Jesus' crucifixion. He is the first of the twelve disciples to see the empty tomb. John is the disciple whom Jesus asks to take His mother, Mary, into John's home (John 19:25–27). I've always wondered why Jesus expected John to take care of His mother, rather than His brothers. Jesus must have felt close to John. Some scholars believe that John was Jesus' cousin, the son of Mary's sister.

Note that Jesus never shows special affection for Judas or cultivates a close relationship with him.

Jesus prays for His disciples. John 17:6–19 is the most moving example of Jesus' prayers for His disciples, prayed before He is arrested:

> For I gave them the words you gave me and they accepted them. They knew with certainty that I came from you, and they believed that you sent

> me. I pray for them. I am not praying for the
> world, but for those you have given me, for they
> are yours. (vv. 8–9)

Jesus prays for God to protect His disciples as He sends them into the world. While Jesus was with them, He protected them and kept them safe (v. 12). Now it's as if the parent is letting go of His children. Jesus will no longer be physically with the disciples to offer protection. He entrusts them to His Father's care. Every parent of adult children understands the pleading prayers we offer to God to protect our children when they have left home and are out of our sight.

Jesus listens to His disciples and calmly deals with arguments, conflicts, and problems at a later time in private, never in the heat of the moment. Mark 9:33–37 reads,

> They came to Capernaum. When he was in the house, he asked them, "What were you arguing about on the road?" But they kept quiet because on the way they had argued about who was the greatest. Sitting down, Jesus called the Twelve and said, "If anyone wants to be first, he must be the very last, and the servant of all. He took a little child and had him stand among them. Taking him in his arms, he said to them, "Whoever welcomes one of these little children in my name welcomes me; and whoever welcomes me does not welcome me but the one who sent me."

In this familiar account, Jesus models how to resolve conflict. God incarnate does not ask questions because He does not know the answer; He asks the disciples questions to start a discussion with them. He gives them the chance to explain ("What were you arguing about on the road?"). He is ready to listen to them.

The disciples argued on the road to Capernaum but Jesus waits until they arrive at the house and sit down to relax before beginning the discussion. Then Jesus uses the example of a child who He takes into His arms. Jesus knows that lectures and mere talk do not make an impression. He always tries to employ a concrete memory image.

Jesus' approach teaches us to:

1. Ask questions first and give children the chance to explain their position.
2. Listen to them.
3. Wait until the incident has passed and privately discuss the problem later when everyone is more relaxed. Lecturing or arguing in the heat of the moment is rarely productive.
4. Use concrete examples and images to illustrate one's position. Mental pictures create the strongest memories.

Jesus is an expert teacher, mentor, encourager, and nurturer, yet even His methods don't appear to be successful all the time. (Please remember that the disciples are people in progress; their story is not finished.) Soon after the above incident occurs, where Jesus clearly states, "Whoever welcomes one of these little children in my name welcomes me," the disciples rebuke parents who brought their children to Jesus for His touch (Mark 10:13–15). They just don't get it. Jesus tells the disciples, "Let the little children come to me . . . Anyone who will not receive the kingdom of God like a little child will never enter it" (vv. 14–15). The disciples cannot transfer the lessons of one experience to another situation. And they certainly don't comprehend that they are also Jesus' little children.

You would imagine that Jesus' teaching had put an end to the disciples' competitive arguments and their jockeying for position. But the brothers, James and John, ask Jesus for a favor, to sit at His right and left hand in glory (Mark 10:37). They know that they are in Jesus' inner circle. The other ten disciples naturally become upset with the brothers for asking that, and argue once again. Most disturbing is that James and John made this request of Jesus just *after* He explained to them that He would soon be killed (Mark 10:32–34). You can hear them thinking, "Now how could this affect us?" instead of focusing on the pain that Jesus will endure. James and John are the same men who will fall asleep in the Garden of Gethsemane on the night Jesus was betrayed.

Imagine that you tell your adult children that you have an aggressive form of cancer, and that you have only a few weeks to live. They are too tired or busy to drive you to your chemotherapy appointments but they do ask, "What arrangements have you made for us after your death? What have you left us in your will?" and then argue among themselves. Jesus was fully divine and fully human, and He must have felt disappointment in His adult children.

THE RISEN CHRIST

You would think that Jesus' resurrection would change everything, that the greatest miracle in human history would transform the disciples immediately into the remarkable men that they will become. Yet the risen Christ continues to parent His disciples when He visits them. Review Jesus' parenting principles and then read John chapter 21. This is Jesus' third visit since His resurrection. He no longer needs to prove to His disciples that He is alive. I think that Jesus continues to visit them because He loves them and genuinely enjoys spending time with them and taking care of them. As always, Jesus begins by asking a question, "Friends, have you caught anything?" (v. 5 NEB).

Jesus shows His disciples where to catch a large load of fish and John recognizes His Lord. Jesus has a fire ready on the beach with fish cooking and some bread. He says to His disciples, "Come and have breakfast" (v. 12), and He serves them the meal. Then Jesus talks to Peter about his coming ministry through asking, "Do you love me?" He specifically explains to Peter the future he faces. In the midst of the discussion, Peter has hurt feelings and even asks

Jesus, "Lord, what about him?" (v. 21, referring to John). Jesus replies, "You must follow me" (v. 22), making it clear that John's future is not Peter's concern.

Even as the risen Christ, the perfect model for parenting is feeding His disciples, asking questions and leading them in discussion, being honest with them about the future, mediating conflicts and jealousies, and spending time with them.

> HE APPEARED TO THEM OVER A PERIOD OF FORTY DAYS AND SPOKE ABOUT THE KINGDOM OF GOD. ON ONE OCCASION, WHILE HE WAS EATING WITH THEM, HE GAVE THEM THIS COMMAND: "DO NOT LEAVE JERUSALEM, BUT WAIT FOR THE GIFT MY FATHER PROMISED, WHICH YOU HAVE HEARD ME SPEAK ABOUT. FOR JOHN BAPTIZED WITH WATER, BUT IN A FEW DAYS YOU WILL BE BAPTIZED WITH THE HOLY SPIRIT."
>
> ACTS 1:3–5

After watching Jesus ascend to heaven at the Mount of Olives, His followers returned to Jerusalem, where "they all joined together constantly in prayer, along with the women and Mary the mother of Jesus, and with his brothers" (Acts 1:14). Remember that the disciples' story is not over; they have been people in progress. They are about to be radically transformed from fearful, confused, dull children into mature, courageous, strong, bold, and committed adult men who are empowered with God's Holy Spirit and willing to sacrifice their lives. In Acts 16:6–7, we read that the Holy Spirit is the Spirit of Jesus, the living, active Spirit who guides His followers, and guides us today.

Any parent of adult children appreciates the long process Jesus engaged in to nurture His disciples, never giving up on them. The disciples have grown up. They have been fully launched and so has the church of Jesus Christ. Too often we simply credit the disciples' transformation with being empowered by the Holy Spirit without remembering the time and love Jesus invested in them. *The Holy Spirit is the Spirit of Jesus.* His presence remained with His disciples, continuing the intimate relationship He developed with them on earth. When you read the rest of the New Testament, remember the disciples as young men whom Jesus personally nurtured.

IN REVIEW

Before covering the foundation blocks for friendship presented in the next chapter, let us review Jesus' parenting method:

1. Jesus made time for His disciples.
2. Jesus understood and provided for His disciples' physical needs.
3. Jesus did not become angry with His disciples, though He was frustrated with them at times.
4. Jesus was a guide, not an authoritarian parent figure.
5. Jesus was open and honest, preparing His disciples for the future.
6. Jesus defended His disciples when the religious establishment criticized them.
7. Jesus enjoyed intimacy with His favorite disciples and made them feel special to Him.
8. Jesus prayed for His disciples.
9. Jesus listened to His disciples and calmly dealt with arguments, conflicts, and problems at a later time in private, never in the heat of the moment.

HOW GREAT IS THE LOVE THE FATHER HAS LAVISHED ON US, THAT WE SHOULD BE CALLED CHILDREN OF GOD! AND THAT IS WHAT WE ARE!

1 JOHN 3:1

WHEN THEY SAW THE COURAGE OF PETER AND JOHN AND REALIZED THAT THEY WERE UNSCHOOLED, ORDINARY MEN, THEY WERE ASTONISHED AND THEY TOOK NOTE THAT THESE MEN HAD BEEN WITH JESUS.

ACTS 4:13

A mother shares:

My husband and I are close friends with our three adult sons. We stopped hands-on parenting when our sons reached eighteen years of age. The only parenting book we have read is God's Word. Every guideline we need is right there. My husband is a policeman who has worked in public schools. We were aware that policemen's children, similar to pastors' kids, can sometimes struggle and rebel. We wanted to be proactive in building solid relationships with our sons. The key has been consistently respecting them since they were young children and understanding them as the unique people God created.

My father had a military career, so I grew up listening to soldiers. I learned that young men are vulnerable. They need understanding and respect, never condemnation. Their voices need to be heard. Our household rules were clear. My husband and sons could wrestle like crazy (I learned not to display fragile items in our home) but none of us were allowed to verbally assault one another. Cruel words can do much more damage because they attack a person made in God's image. I tried to protect my sons' areas of weakness from public view until they were mature enough to handle those challenges. Home can be a safe place for boys as they grow into men.

My husband has been an outstanding, godly role model for our sons. He never succumbed to our culture's belief that "kids always come first" and the family should be worshiped. He made it clear that God comes first. God runs our family. We follow our Lord. The best way to guide children is to always be the hands and feet of Jesus.

We have been a sanctuary for our sons to share their problems. We are here to help them, listen to them, pray for them, unconditionally love them, be compassionate, and never condemn them. Sin is between them and God. God knows their hearts. We are equal brothers and sisters in Christ. Our sons' friends often come to talk to us about their problems. When a local pastor's daughter could not tell her parents that she was pregnant, she came to us.

We never told our children to avoid bad influences. We want our kids to influence and minister to hurting young people. Since we are involved in youth ministry, our sons bring different friends to our home for worship, music, and good discussions. Our sons are musicians. Making music as a family has always been one of our core activities.

Our lives have not been perfect. Sometimes we've financially struggled, when my husband was out of work. But while we were not able to supply our children with ample money and possessions, we did give them an abundance of our time, love, and grace.

A mother shares:

Last night my adult son stopped by our home. He sat on the couch and poured out his heart, talking about his latest challenges. I thought of all the advice and solutions I could offer him but I kept my mouth shut and listened. I realize that this is why he comes to talk to me. Sometimes I do offer suggestions, but never as criticism. I tell him that I struggle with similar problems and discuss ways that I cope.

We recently ate dinner at our daughter's home. She and her husband have hectic work schedules and the kitchen was messy, filled with dirty dishes from previous meals. As I sat in their home, I thought that perhaps I should clean their kitchen and wash all those dishes. Wouldn't that help them? But then I asked myself, "Would I do that in a friend's house?" No, I would simply enjoy my friend's company and be grateful for the gift of hospitality. So I relaxed, ignored the mess, and enjoyed time with my children.

There have always been friendships between mothers and daughters. Today, because of the lack of a generation gap and the overlap in clothing, books, music, and movie tastes, mother-daughter friendships may appear to be more common. However, the primary responsibility of a mother to be a role model and source of advice for and comfort to her daughters remains the same.

Linda Gordon and Susan Shaffer

A beautiful statue can be created by either starting with a large piece of marble and chipping away or starting with a lump of clay and building up. Although in the art world either method may produce a beautiful work, in the parenting world the chipping method is unproductive. We pronounce what our children are doing wrong rather than what they are doing right. We correct rather than teach. To raise resilient children, parents must understand that one of their most important roles is to be a disciplinarian in the true sense. The word discipline relates to the word disciple and thus is a teaching process.

Robert Brooks and Sam Goldstein

THREE

Laying the Foundation
for Friendship

THE RAIN CAME DOWN, THE STREAMS
ROSE, AND THE WINDS BLEW AND BEAT
AGAINST THAT HOUSE; YET IT DID NOT FALL,
BECAUSE IT HAD ITS FOUNDATION ON THE
ROCK. BUT EVERYONE WHO HEARS THESE
WORDS OF MINE AND DOES NOT PUT THEM
INTO PRACTICE IS LIKE A FOOLISH MAN WHO
BUILT HIS HOUSE ON SAND. THE RAIN CAME
DOWN, THE STREAMS ROSE, AND THE WINDS
BLEW AND BEAT AGAINST THAT HOUSE, AND
IT FELL WITH A GREAT CRASH.

MATTHEW 7:25–27

Living in the San Francisco Bay area of California, I have experienced several earthquakes. In our more severe quakes, buildings with poor foundations collapse. The buildings that endure severe stress are usually newer buildings, built according to current earthquake codes. When we build a solid foundation for healthy adult friendships with our children, we prevent a disaster when severe stress comes. We are like the wise man who built his house and its foundation on rock. If we don't take the time to build this foundation, our relationships can collapse with a great crash during the storms that life inevitably brings.

As a classroom teacher, principal, and district administrator, Mr. Williams has spent his career nurturing children. He has close friendships with his four adult children and is now enjoying his grandchildren. When asked for parenting advice, he always offers this succinct answer: "Whenever making a decision or taking an action with your child, think about how it will affect your future adult relationship with them. Always keep focused on long-term results." When I asked his adult daughter, a mother of two young children, for her view, she responded, "My dad gave me the best advice. He told my husband and me to raise kids that we would enjoy hanging out with as adults because we will spend many more years with them as adults than kids."

Parents who focus on the future and keep the "long view" in mind have a goal of becoming healthy adult friends with their children. They know that they will reap what they sow. This vision usually avoids the day-to-day mistakes of overparenting or underparenting. This approach can be described as *purposeful parenting*. Parents realize that they are making a lifetime investment in their children, the ultimate retirement account where wise, loving parenting will pay great relational dividends.

Before moving any further, I must clarify that this book does not address relationships with adult children who suffer with mental illness, addictions, or other disorders. Many dedicated parents have done all the right things in raising their children and laid a solid foundation. Yet their adult children struggle and the parent-child relationship remains painful. Several excellent books on this topic are available, such as Bill Coleman's *Parents with Broken Hearts* and Jane Adams's *When Our Grown Kids Disappoint Us*.

Two Common Threads

I interviewed many parents and adult children for this book. In the midst of countless wonderful insights and ideas, two common threads emerged in almost every discussion. Adult children who are good friends with their parents consistently told me:

> I can tell my parents anything. They simply listen and do not judge me. I can be honest with them. They are always there for me. I enjoy hanging out with them. Even if they were not my parents, I would still choose to spend time with them.

Parents who are good friends with their children consistently told me:

> This is the best stage of having children. Of course, I love my adult children, but I also *like* them. They are interesting people. I respect them and enjoy spending time with them. I am happy to be a trusted advisor instead of a 24/7 parent. I ask them for advice too. Even if they were not my children, I would choose to spend time with them.

One clear sign of a great friendship is that both parents and children initiate opportunities to spend time together. They choose to be close friends. These strong friendships did not occur overnight. Parents laid building blocks for them when children were young. They cultivated future friendship by establishing practices early that continued through the turbulent teen years and undergirded their children's path to adulthood. What follow are eighteen foundation blocks that purposeful parents laid to nurture future friendship with their children. Observe the similarities between these principles and Jesus' methods listed in chapter 2.

FOUNDATION BLOCK #1: PROTECTION

> **A STRONG MAN WHO TRUSTS IN THE FEAR OF THE LORD WILL BE A REFUGE FOR HIS SONS.**
>
> PROVERBS 14:26 NEB

Parents who become friends with their adult children do *not* start out as friends. When children are growing up, parents are not buddies or peers but their children's protectors, caretakers, providers, guides, teachers, and trustworthy models. They daily live out a concrete illustration of our heavenly Father. We know that the core of a child's understanding of God our Father begins with his or her experience with a human parent. Trust is learned.

Lucy and her young divorced mom were buddies. During Lucy's teen years, Lucy and her mom often shopped and went to the movies on school nights, ignoring Lucy's homework deadlines. When Lucy began experimenting with alcohol, drugs, and sex, her mom was her confidante. They would even share dating stories. Lucy's mom wanted to be her buddy, not her parent. Kathleen's mother suffered with mental illness and was a prescription drug addict. When her father was at work, Kathleen took care of her mother and brother. She often went home from school at lunchtime to make sure that her mother had not overdosed. Lindsey's parents were both alcoholics. She took care of her younger siblings and tried her best to stop her parents from driving when they were drunk. Stacey's mother was either at work or asleep when her stepfather regularly approached her to have sex. Greg was sexually abused for years by a close family friend who was a member of the clergy. Today none of these adults are friends with their parents. When Greg's parents pleaded with him to have a relationship, saying, "But we didn't know," he responded, "You should have known or tried to find out. You should have protected me." Greg has not had contact with his parents for years and intends to never speak to them again.

Purposeful parents ferociously protect their children's safety when they are young. They provide for their children and take care of their needs, not expecting or allowing their children to care for them or parent their siblings. They are unafraid to set boundaries and limits, no matter how unpopular it makes them. They take their roles as guide and teacher seriously and realize that they are their child's number-one role model in following God. These parents understand that they are stewards of a precious treasure, entrusted to them by God. As Proverbs 3:12 says, "For Yahweh reproves the man he loves, as a father checks a well-loved son" (JB).

FOUNDATION BLOCK #2: INDIVIDUAL TIME

> I TOO WAS ONCE A SON WITH A FATHER, IN MY MOTHER'S EYES A TENDER CHILD, UNIQUE.
>
> PROVERBS 4:3 JB

Parents who later become friends with their adult children are intentional about spending time with their young children to develop unique, special relationships. These parents give the gift of time and availability. They are not rushed or distracted when spending time with their children. They are fully present. Children know that they are a top priority, not an inconvenience. These parents treat each child as an individual, respecting him or her as a unique creation of God, and tell their children that they are special for who they are, not for what they do. They not only accept their children's differences, but celebrate them.

Purposeful parents spend time alone with each child in the family. Each parent has a special relationship with each child, separate from the spouse's relationship. As much father/daughter time is carved out as mother/daughter time, and mother/son time as father/son time. Saturday brunch is connection time for the McAllister family, as Jackie and Kurt rotate having breakfast with their children at their favorite restaurants. John and his son have season tickets to the local baseball stadium, and John takes his daughter to ballet performances. When John's children became teenagers and began distancing themselves from him, they still chose to attend these events together. Kevin traveled for a living and took each of his children on different business trips during the year.

Ryan has always taken his sons on annual camping trips. As adolescence approached, Isabel took each of her daughters on a weekend trip to the beach to informally discuss the physical and emotional changes they would soon experience. She offered them a safe place to ask questions and shared what God's Word said.'

Some of the opportunities to spend one-on-one time with children happen naturally in families as members go in different directions, while special activities or trips need to be scheduled. The specific plans are irrelevant. What is most important is that parents develop a habit of spending individual time with their children that will continue into adulthood. The young child who wanted to go out for ice cream to talk with mom or dad will still want to go out for dessert and discussion as an adult.

FOUNDATION BLOCK #3: FAMILY TIME

> **FAMILIES WHO TREASURE THEIR TRADITIONS AND RITUALS SEEM AUTOMATICALLY TO HAVE A SENSE OF FAMILY. TRADITIONS ARE THE UNDERPINNING IN SUCH FAMILIES, REGARDED AS NECESSITIES NOT FRILLS.**
>
> DOLORES CURRAN

Parents who become friends with their adult children value and protect family time. They guard their daily dinner hour as much as they guard major holiday events. They include their own parents and extended family in celebrations, modeling how to treat older relatives for their children. Children learn how to treat their parents by watching how mom and dad treat *their* parents. Purposeful parents communicate that their children's presence is welcomed and enjoyed, never simply tolerated. They look for ways to connect and celebrate their children through special rituals. Numerous traditions are woven into the fabric of their families. They understand that family rituals are not frivolous extras, but the glue of family life. My favorite example of this occurred when close friends were estranged from their adult son. Marie had always served pumpkin soup during Halloween week. Her son was struggling with serious problems. Marie and her husband had not heard from him in months. They were shocked when he appeared at their door, telling them, "I'm here for pumpkin soup." Many parents tell stories of estranged children unexpectedly showing up for family traditions. The glue holds when it is most needed. Susan Lieberman says, "Tradition is family insurance against outside pressures that threaten to overwhelm our days and weaken our ties to each other."[1]

While some parents plan trips as opportunities to get away from their kids, purposeful parents plan events and trips to spend more time with their children and build memories. They initiate ways to spend time together, and when their children become adults, the children initiate plans to spend time with their parents.

While foundation block #2 encourages us to spend time developing individual relationships, foundation block #3 shows us that protecting family time and traditions is equally important.

FOUNDATION BLOCK #4: SAFE HAVEN

WE FIND A HOME FOR OUR HEART WHEN WE ARE
SAFE AND KNOW OUR VOICES WILL BE HEARD.

CHARLOTTE SOPHIA KASL

Parents who become friends with their adult children plan specific times when children can share their concerns and feelings without judgment. They create a safe place for their children to be honest. These parents focus on listening and communicate that their children are heard. Some parents plan family meetings, while others find one-on-one time to be more effective. During these safe haven times, parents do not react, critique, correct, instruct, discipline, become angry, or interrogate. If they ask questions, they do so to better understand their children's views. They try to see an issue through their child's eyes. They simply listen and keep what is said confidential. When they need to correct and discipline, they do this at a different time.

Many purposeful parents designate dinnertime as their family safe haven. Arguments, correction, criticism, interrogation, and disciplinary action are barred from dinner table conversation. In our home, our children nicknamed our safe haven "Trust Time." Before they fell asleep in their beds, I told them that they could tell God and me anything before we prayed and we would simply listen. I called it "Truce Time" but they didn't understand that phrase. They renamed it "Trust Time," which seemed more fitting anyway. I wanted them to learn that they could bring any concern to God their Father and He would hear them.

Deborah told me, "I grew up knowing that it was always safe to tell my parents the truth. They said that I would never be in trouble for anything I did wrong if I was honest with them first." When one of Robert's kids was having a bad day and seemed unusually upset, Robert would take his child out for "sundae vent time." As they ate ice cream sundaes, Robert simply listened as his child vented and shared problems. When there was a break in conversation, Robert would calmly ask, "And what else?" When his child was done venting and had calmed down, Robert helped clear up misunderstandings and brainstormed solutions. Usually the venting alone solved the perceived problem, and the ice cream sundae helped too.

Several parents have found writing letters and interactive journaling to be effective ways to nurture safe communication without judgment. This approach will be covered in chapter 4.

You may remember that many adult children who enjoy friendships with their parents told me, "I can tell my parents anything. They don't judge me and simply listen." These children have no reason to lie or withhold information. This relationship of trust began as small moments of safe haven time, glimpses of a future friendship, and developed into an adult relationship where all communication is safe and honest. Adult friends do not correct, discipline, critique, overreact, or interrogate each other. More important, children have learned that they can feel safe in being honest with God, completely trusting Him.

FOUNDATION BLOCK #5: GIFT OF CHILDHOOD

DELAY PLAY AND DELAY ADULTHOOD.

HARA MARANO

Parents who become friends with their adult children give them the gift of childhood. They allow them to be children, not mini-adults. They do not over-schedule or over-manage them. They encourage their children to play and explore. I grew up living on a cul-de-sac. As I played with other neighborhood kids in our cul-de-sac, my mom watched us through the kitchen window. She certainly intervened in our play if we were in danger or someone was hurt, but mostly she and the other moms left us alone. On summer days, we played all kinds of games, often late into the night. Our favorite one was hide-and-seek. We organized sports games in the cul-de-sac without adult coaches. We rode our bikes and roller-skated. When we were bored, we created elaborate pretend games. We also wrote and performed plays, complete with scenery and costumes. Such productions could keep us busy for days. We learned how to lead and follow. We learned to get along and compromise when we didn't agree, without adult intervention. When we were bored, our parents said, "Go find something to do." They didn't sign us up for another class. Our parents didn't arrange playdates.

Many of our children, including my own, did not experience this freedom in childhood. My children grew up in a home that was located on a busy corner with high traffic. None of the neighborhood children played outside. I tried to provide my children with a similar experience of independent exploration and play in the safety of our home, and I hope that many other parents did as well. I hope we allowed them to be children when appropriate so that they were ready to embrace adulthood.

FOUNDATION BLOCK #6: DREAM CATCHING

> CHILDREN REQUIRE HOPE AND COURAGE TO FOLLOW THEIR GOALS. THESE QUALITIES HELP THEM DEVELOP THE INNER STRENGTH AND RESILIENCE NECESSARY TO SUCCEED DESPITE THE ADVERSITIES THAT MAY AND OFTEN DO COME THEIR WAY.
>
> ROBERT BROOKS AND SAM GOLDSTEIN

Parents who become friends with their adult children embrace their children's dreams and passions. They are their children's most enthusiastic cheerleaders. They try to attend every activity and event to cheer their children on. Purposeful parents applaud the differences in their children. They observe each child's natural bent and encourage them to pursue it. PeggySue describes her role as a "dream catcher," helping her children to follow their passions and live out their dreams. She explains: "First I listen carefully to their desires and dreams. Then I cultivate loving what they love, whether it is racing horses or playing a musical instrument. Without being intrusive, my job is to remove obstacles for them. I listen to them and then ask, 'How can I help?'"

Helping children to pursue their dreams is radically different from burdening them with the parents' dreams. Lydia was a true musical prodigy. Her mother dreamed that she would become a concert pianist. Lydia had the rare gifts necessary to achieve that goal. Yet when Lydia graduated from high school, she turned down acceptances to the best conservatories in the nation. She didn't touch the piano again. She tried to explain to her mother that they didn't share the same dream but her mother refused to listen.

FOUNDATION BLOCK #7: LEVEL PLAYING FIELD

CHILDREN WHO ARE BOUND BY BIOLOGICAL OR LEGAL TIES CAN CLAIM THE TITLE OF FAMILY; BUT TO ACTUALLY BE A FAMILY . . . REQUIRES A COMMITMENT TO SPENDING A GOOD AMOUNT OF TIME IN THE PURSUIT OF NOTHING MORE THAN BEING TOGETHER.

JOHN ROSEMOND

Parents who become friends with their adult children find ways to be on a level playing field when appropriate. When their children are young, these parents get down on the floor and play games with them, acting as playmates. They laugh and are silly. These parents take a break from being teaching, correcting parents. When the children became older, they learn a shared hobby together. They are on equal footing as students and often the children learn faster than their parents, giving children the chance to encourage and teach their parents.

Richard and his sons play in a band together. Jack and his teenage son took scuba diving lessons and now travel for annual dive trips. Janice and her son race sailboats. Camille and her daughter pursued piano lessons together. Kyle taught his children to play golf and now they regularly beat him. Families enjoy sharing an activity and spending time together. Parents take a hiatus from their daily parenting role and become peer participants. Learning new skills can develop into shared family hobbies that can last for a lifetime.

FOUNDATION BLOCK #8: LAUGHTER

> **HUMOR IS THE SHORTEST DISTANCE BETWEEN TWO PEOPLE.**
>
> VICTOR BORGE

Parents who become friends with their adult children frequently laugh together. They don't take themselves too seriously. Public speakers and teachers know that humor is the most effective teaching tool. When we learn information while laughing, we remember it. Laughter releases "feel good chemicals" in our bodies, and the benefits of laughter can actually equal the benefits of cardiovascular aerobic exercise. Laughter therapy is even prescribed for recovering hospital patients. Supporting the familiar adage, "Laughter is the best medicine," Proverbs 17:22 states: "A glad heart is excellent medicine, a spirit depressed wastes the bones away" (JB).

Pure and simple, we like to be with people who make us laugh. Families who laugh a lot want to be together. The authors of *Emotionally Intelligent Parenting* explain:

> We think that laughter is missing from the lives of too many families, and that it's the single thing that can really make a difference in terms of creating a caring, problem-solving environment. Families that laugh together can enjoy one another's company, put ideas forward that might not be perfect or well thought out, make mistakes

without being afraid of being ridiculed—and, believe it or not, they are healthier for it. We can light up our lives by lightening up our households.[2]

FOUNDATION BLOCK #9: SEEING THE HEART

> HE SAID TO THEM, "YOU ARE THE ONES WHO JUSTIFY YOURSELVES IN THE EYES OF MEN, BUT GOD KNOWS YOUR HEARTS."
>
> LUKE 16:15

Parents who become friends with their adult children clearly communicate guidelines for expected behavior based solely on biblical principles. These parents do not confuse biblical behavior with their own desires or cultural expectations. They understand that God sees the heart and cares about their children's character, not their appearance or personal preferences. Purposeful parents are not influenced by the opinions of friends and relatives who disapprove of their children's external choices about tattoos, piercings, clothes, hair color, or music. They verbalize their loyalty to their children and do not participate in the criticism. Yet they do not bend on biblical character issues.

Most parents realize that discipline is most effective within the context of an intimate, loving relationship, where the child respects and trusts the parent. This is how God loves and guides us. One parent established these guidelines as the Golden Rules of the Household:

> Love God and your neighbor as yourself. Refrain from behavior that is illegal, unbiblical, immoral, unethical, and life-threatening. Everything else is up for discussion.

FOUNDATION BLOCK #10: KEEPING CONFIDENCES

> A TITTLE-TATTLER LETS SECRETS OUT, A TRUST-
> WORTHY MAN KEEPS THINGS HIDDEN.
>
> PROVERBS 11:13 JB

Parents who become friends with their adult children keep their children's confidences. Jocelyn says, "Whenever I share something with my mom, it goes into the vault." In contrast, Amber explains, "I could never trust my mom. If I shared something with her when I was a teenager, I soon heard her telling her friends about it on the phone. The worst was when some of her friends were the mothers of my friends. Today if I tell her about a problem I'm experiencing, she tells my siblings about it within a few days."

Purposeful parents practice direct communication. They do not send messages through other family members. They do not discuss one child's problems with another child. They do not inquire of siblings about a brother's or sister's life. They speak directly to their child.

Gossiping about one's child should not be confused with sharing one's struggles in confidence with a trusted friend or one's spouse. Every parent needs a supportive friend and trustworthy confidante with whom struggles can be shared and ways to help the child can be brainstormed.

FOUNDATION BLOCK #11: PRAYER

> WE CAN APPROACH GOD WITH CONFIDENCE FOR
> THIS REASON: IF WE MAKE REQUESTS WHICH
> ACCORD WITH HIS WILL HE LISTENS TO US; AND
> IF WE KNOW THAT OUR REQUESTS ARE HEARD,

> WE KNOW ALSO THAT THE THINGS WE ASK FOR
> ARE OURS.
>
> 1 JOHN 5:14–15 NEB

Parents who become friends with their adult children have always prayed for them. As adults, their children know that they can come to them with any struggle and ask for prayer. They bring friends who need guidance and prayer. These parents know that they can't fix their children's lives but they can always pray. Mary Emily told me, "Prayer is the key to trusting God and letting go of our adult children. The less we can say, the more we should pray. This is critical when we are concerned about their choices." Purposeful parents also understand that they are praying for God's best for their children, not for what they perceive is best for their children. First John 5:14–15 tells us that God listens to us if we make requests which accord with His will. We must align our vision with God's vision. Abraham Lincoln wisely said, "Don't ever think that God is on your side. Pray earnestly that you are on God's side."

Throughout Acts, we read several examples of Jesus' Spirit guiding Paul and his companions, stopping them from preaching in certain areas and leading them to others (see Acts 16:6–10). This same living Christ leads our children today. When we pray for our children, we are praying for Christ to guide them. He knows how to work out His purposes in their lives better than we do.

FOUNDATION BLOCK #12: BIBLICAL EXAMPLE

> TRAIN UP A CHILD IN THE WAY HE SHOULD GO—
> AND WALK THERE YOURSELF ONCE IN A WHILE.
>
> JOSH BILLINGS

Parents who become friends with their adult children hold themselves to the same biblical standards they hope their children will follow. These children know that their parents are trustworthy, consistent, and can be counted on to follow Christ in word and deed. Even when they disagree with their parents, they respect and trust them. Lisa told me, "I don't need to preach at my children. My life speaks much louder. We parents can be important role models without saying one word."

FOUNDATION BLOCK #13: UNCONDITIONAL LOVE

> **LORD, PLEASE HELP ME TO REMEMBER TO TREAT MY CHILDREN AS YOU TREAT ME . . . WITH LOVE, GRACE, AND LOTS OF MERCY.**
>
> GIGI GRAHAM TCHIVIDJIAN

Parents who become friends with their adult children have communicated their unconditional love for their children since birth. One dad told me, "How do my children know that I love them? Because I tell them!" These purposeful parents have always been there for their children. Their children know that they are deeply loved, even when they make mistakes or poor choices. As they approach adulthood, their parents tell them that they will be their safety net and they will never go hungry. Usually this security gives children the confidence to reach for their dreams and take risks to achieve success in adulthood.

FOUNDATION BLOCK #14: HONESTY

> **A STRAIGHTFORWARD ANSWER IS AS GOOD AS A KISS OF FRIENDSHIP.**
>
> PROVERBS 24:26 NEB

Parents who become friends with their adult children have been consistently truthful. They practice honest communication, with no pretense or mixed messages. What they say is what they mean. Purposeful parents can admit to making a mistake and are able to say "I'm sorry" to their children. They can seek forgiveness from their children and generously offer it. When appropriate and helpful, they are not afraid to admit their own failings and struggles. They do not pretend to be perfect or have all the answers.

FOUNDATION BLOCK #15: MUTUAL RESPECT

> HE THAT WILL HAVE HIS SON HAVE A RESPECT
> FOR HIM AND HIS ORDERS, MUST HIMSELF HAVE
> A GREAT REVERENCE FOR HIS SON.
>
> JOHN LOCKE

Parents who become friends with their adult children have sown the seeds of mutual respect. Respect and trust are earned. Purposeful parents teach their children to respect others by treating them with respect. They speak with respect. They are up front with their children and do not manipulate behind the scenes. They respect their privacy, knocking before opening a closed bedroom door. They do not open their children's mail or investigate their electronic life. They show their children that they trust them. Purposeful parents expect their children to return the respect.

Remember that this book does not address helping children with addictions and other struggles. Parents must use their discretion about privacy when their children's lives are in danger.

FOUNDATION BLOCK #16: LETTING GO

> GOOD JUDGMENT AND THE POWER TO MAKE
> THE RIGHT DECISIONS DON'T SPRING FULL

BLOWN; THEY HAVE TO BE TRAINED, PRACTICED, REHEARSED IN COUNTLESS LITTLE DECISIONS THROUGH CHILDHOOD.

HARA MARANO

Parents who become friends with their adult children understand that the goal of parenting is to let go. They do not let go overnight but in gradual stages according to the child's age. They let their young children make mistakes and learn to solve problems on their own. They do not bail out their teenagers, realizing that making mistakes and suffering the consequences of one's actions are often life's best teachers. Purposeful parents teach their children to be financially independent by expecting them to earn money to pay for a desired goal, whether they are earning money for a school trip, paying for car insurance, or contributing toward college tuition.

Purposeful parents understand that every important life skill requires practice. When parents constantly intervene to fix problems, they deprive their children of practice in problem solving and perseverance. We would not expect our children to learn to play a musical instrument or excel in a sport without daily practice. Of course, parents would prefer that their children learn tough life lessons in the safety of their home surrounded by a loving family, but this is not always possible. Isabel says, "The key to letting go of my children is remembering that their successes are not my successes, nor are their failures my failures."

Purposeful parents never make children feel guilty for separating from the family and becoming independent. They encourage their children to practice becoming adults. Letting go is essential to becoming adult friends, so this topic will be covered further in chapter 6.

Purposeful parents do not enable their children. Yet they are not reckless, ignoring life-threatening consequences. They know how to find help for their children in dangerous situations.

FOUNDATION BLOCK #17: FAITH JOURNEY

> IF ANYONE COMES TO ME AND DOES NOT HATE
> HIS FATHER AND MOTHER, HIS WIFE AND CHIL-
> DREN, HIS BROTHERS AND SISTERS—YES, EVEN
> HIS OWN LIFE—HE CANNOT BE MY DISCIPLE.
> AND ANYONE WHO DOES NOT CARRY HIS CROSS
> AND FOLLOW ME CANNOT BE MY DISCIPLE.
>
> LUKE 14:26–27

Jesus' strong words remind us that faith is not inherited. We want our children to follow Jesus Christ, not us. Parents who become friends with their adult children allow children to take their own journey of faith and develop their relationship with God separate from their parents' relationship with Him. Purposeful parents let go in this area and do not try to micromanage their child's spiritual life. They allow them to explore attending other churches, experience other worship styles, and view different interpretations of Scripture.

These parents are open to God's calling in their child's life, especially when it is different from their vision for their child's life. They respect their child's response to God.

Some parents who forced their children to attend their home church realized too late that they won the battle but lost the war. Focusing on church attendance instead of a deepening relationship with Christ resulted in their children walking away from both.

FOUNDATION BLOCK #18: WEIGHING OUR WORDS

> THE TONGUE THAT SOOTHES IS A TREE OF LIFE;
> THE BARBED TONGUE, A BREAKER OF HEARTS.
>
> PROVERBS 15:4 JB

Parents who become friends with their adult children carefully weigh their words. Since this is one of the most important foundation blocks to a healthy adult friendship, this topic will be covered in-depth in the next chapter. A pattern of careless or cruel remarks can ruin a potential friendship.

IN REVIEW

In reading this chapter, it probably occurred to you, as it did to me, that these principles are simply wise parenting techniques for developing good relationships with growing children. This is precisely the point: The foundation we lay to have healthy relationships with our growing children will allow us to have healthy adult friendships. These habits are established when our children are young. A close adult friendship with our children does not happen overnight. The seeds are sown in childhood.

Keeping in mind Jesus' principles for building relationships with His disciples (from the previous chapter), let us review the foundation blocks for building healthy adult friendships with one's children.

Parents who enjoy healthy adult friendships with their grown children:

#1   Protected and cared for their children.

#2   Spent individual time with each of their children.

#3   Made spending time as a family a priority, guarding rituals and traditions.

#4   Created a safe haven where they simply listened and their children could tell them anything without being judged.

#5   Gave their children the gift of childhood, without over-managing their lives.

#6   Encouraged their children to pursue their passions and dreams.

#7   Found ways to be on a level playing field and learned new skills together.

#8   Laughed a lot together.

#9   Saw their children's hearts as God does, basing their behavioral expectations on biblical principles, not personal preferences.

#10   Kept their children's confidences and practiced direct communication.

#11   Prayed for their children, trusting them to God's will.

#12   Committed to be a biblical example for their children in following God.

#13   Communicated that they unconditionally loved their children.

#14   Were honest with their children about their own mistakes and failings and could apologize to their children and ask for forgiveness.

#15   Nurtured mutual respect. Unless they were concerned about their children's safety, they respected their privacy and trusted them.

#16   Allowed their children to make mistakes and learn from them. They always understood that the ultimate goal of parenting was to help their children become independent adults.

#17   Allowed their children to take their own journey of faith in following God's calling and purpose in their lives.

#18   Weighed their words carefully.

CHILDREN NEED MORE THAN FOOD, SHELTER, AND CLOTHING. THEY NEED AT LEAST ONE PERSON WHO IS CRAZY ABOUT THEM.

FRAN STOTT

A father shares:

I really don't know why my wife and I have the privilege of being close friends with our adult children. I know plenty of parents who have lost touch with their kids and I ache for them.

I remember making a decision when our children were young that we would never ask them, "Where did you get an idea like that?" My own parents often asked that question, usually at the dinner table, with a tone that suggested my ideas and those of my three siblings were off-limits or improper, certainly not welcomed. My parents didn't realize that their efforts to control our dinner table conversation resulted only in a guarded reticence on my part that affected my communication with them for years. My wife and I decided to welcome our children's ideas, never stifle them, especially at the dinner table. We also wanted to focus on building relationships. Through daily conversation, our children learned who we were as people, how we followed God, and what we valued. We didn't have to orchestrate "teachable moments."

Many parents would consider it anathema if I suggested that parenting is a collaborative exercise with one's children. I wasn't afraid to be honest with my children. Sometimes when faced with a parenting decision I would tell them, "I don't know. I've never done this before." My authoritarian parents pretended to have all the answers. My wife and I always made the final decision and laid down the law, but we discussed decisions with our kids about curfews, allowances, dating, parties, and other issues. We listened to them first.

We also apologized and asked our children for forgiveness when appropriate. Because offering forgiveness is as sweet as receiving it, I wanted our children to experience that sweetness firsthand at home. Because the strongest friendships for me have been forged in the fiery dramas of failure, confession, forgiveness, and reconciliation, I wanted to nurture a similar friendship with my children.

My wife and I didn't micromanage our children's lives. We stressed the "majors," which were biblical guidelines, but didn't worry about the "minors." We observed too many parents having unnecessary confrontation with their teens about the "minors." It's obvious to me that there is an inverse correlation between friendship and meddling. After our daughter's wedding, I wrote a letter to my son-in-law to convey the same unconditional love with no expectations that I have extended to my children.

Our kids know that they are not perfect nor will they ever be perfect. My wife and I are not perfect parents and won't be perfect grandparents. Through Jesus Christ, that beautiful imperfection is the common denominator that will forever cement our adult friendship.

His adult daughter shares:

I am good friends with my parents and enjoying spending time with them. We thoroughly enjoy each other's company. When I go home to visit, a typical dinner lasts for about four hours. I find it hard to leave the table to go meet other friends. While growing up, family dinner was always an important part of our day, even when our schedules were hectic. My parents never tired of listening to the stories my brother and I told about school and our friends. My parents are still the first people I call when I have great news, a funny story, experience a bad day, or need advice.

Yet my parents were not really my "friends" until I became an independent adult. When I lived at home, I knew that my parents were the rulers of our household and I respected them. They had the final say. Today they have found a good balance in letting me live my own life, yet offering counsel when I need it. Now that I am married and thinking about having my own family, I hope that I can do half the job they did as parents.

An adult daughter shares:

My relationship with my parents is better than a friendship, because they unconditionally love me. If I am having a bad day and need to vent, I call my parents. If I want to share a victory in my life, I call my parents. They are there for me no matter what.

One of the best ways my parents built friend relationships in our family was to take frequent vacations. Whether we were traveling for a weekend or a long trip, we built memories that bonded us together. We laughed a lot. My parents had high expectations of us at home but when we were on vacation, we all broke the rules. My dad would wake us up to eat ice cream in the middle of the night. He called those times "secret midnight snacks." When we were driving home from one vacation, we passed a well-known amusement park. Mom said, "Too bad we don't have time for that. We have to be home today." Dad immediately drove off the freeway, asking, "Why not?" We spent a fun day at the amusement park.

My dad traveled often for business so he rotated taking us children on individual trips with him. These trips were gifts for celebrating birthdays, graduations, and other milestones. My favorite trip was going to New York to see Broadway shows.

When we weren't traveling, we had family sleepovers on Friday nights and went on local adventures on Saturdays. Our friends were always welcome in our home. They became part of our family. They came to our home because it was a fun, creative place.

Today my relationship with my parents is like our vacation relationship. Now we are adult friends. I believe that when people are friends, they become interested in one another's passions. I go to baseball games with my dad and travel on scuba trips with him.

I go to movies and tea time with my mom. Even though we spend family time together, I try to have an individual relationship with each of my parents. Sometimes I plan events for them and initiate seeing them. If kids want to be friends with their parents, I think they need to make an equal effort in pursuing that friendship. It's a two-way street.

Words are clothes that thoughts wear.

Samuel Butler

Words—so innocent and powerless as they are, as standing in a dictionary, how potent for good and evil they become in the hands of one who knows how to combine them.

Nathaniel Hawthorne

My son, keep well thy tongue, and keep thy friend.

Geoffrey Chaucer

FOUR

USING OUR WORDS WISELY

THERE ARE SOME WHOSE THOUGHTLESS
WORDS PIERCE LIKE A SWORD,
BUT THE TONGUE OF THE WISE BRINGS
HEALING.

PROVERBS 12:18 JB

The single most important factor in cultivating and continuing friendships with our adult children is communication: the words that come out of our mouths, what we write, and, equally important, what we don't say. We must practice the ministry of carefully choosing our words. We all know relationships that were destroyed by one cruel, reckless comment. Cruel words are intended to hurt but thoughtless words can inflict equally deep wounds.

Too often people speak kinder to strangers and acquaintances than to their closest family members. Sometimes we think that we have a free pass with our spouses, children, parents, and other relatives to say anything we want. Some Christians even couch this destructive communication habit in spiritual terms by claiming to have the gift of exhortation or discernment. They freely share wisdom and advice (criticism) when it is not requested and believe that they are being helpful.

We are taught such well-known adages as "If you can't say anything nice, then don't say anything at all," and "Once the words come out of your mouth, you can't take them back." These adages acknowledge that words are powerful. What do the Scriptures say about the power of our words? Plenty. As we embark on a biblical crash course on the power of words, ponder how the verses apply to all of your relationships, especially your relationships with your adult children.

Jesus often argued with the Pharisees about what made a person "clean" or "unclean." What goes into our mouths does not make us clean or unclean. What comes out of our mouths reveals our true heart condition.

> DON'T YOU SEE THAT WHATEVER ENTERS THE MOUTH GOES INTO THE STOMACH AND THEN OUT OF THE BODY? BUT THE THINGS THAT COME OUT OF THE MOUTH COME FROM THE HEART, AND THESE MAKE A MAN "UNCLEAN."
>
> MATTHEW 15:17–18

WISE SPEECH

> THE TONGUE HAS POWER OF LIFE AND DEATH; MAKE FRIENDS WITH IT AND ENJOY ITS FRUITS.
>
> PROVERBS 18:21 NEB

Throughout Proverbs, wise speech is contrasted with foolish speech. Proverbs has been called the common sense book of the Bible. While the Psalms focus on our intimate relationship with God, Proverbs teaches us about relating to others. In *The Old Testament Poetic Books*, C. H. Bullock states, "Proverbs is an instructional manual . . . a primer of right conduct and essential attitudes toward life, aimed at producing lives in conformity to the divine will. The immediate object was to train and educate for the preservation of the family unit and social stability."[1] Nurturing healthy family relationships is a key focus in Proverbs. The principles in Proverbs are not difficult to understand. They are difficult to put into daily practice.

The best summary of wise speech is found in Proverbs 10:19–21: "When men talk too much, sin is never far away; common sense holds its tongue. A good man's tongue is pure silver; the heart of the wicked is trash. The lips of a good man teach many, but fools perish for want of sense" (NEB).

Choosing our words wisely is a habit, requiring practice and self-control. According to Proverbs and the New Testament, we practice wise speech when we:

Hold our tongue

- "Keep a guard over your lips and tongue and keep yourself out of trouble" (Proverbs 21:23 NEB).
- "Experience uses few words; discernment keeps a cool head. Even a fool, if he holds his peace, is thought wise; keep your mouth shut and show your good sense" (Proverbs 17:27–28 NEB).
- "If anyone considers himself religious and yet does not keep a tight rein on his tongue, he deceives himself and his religion is worthless" (James 1:26).

Use our words to share knowledge and increase learning

- "The wise man's mind guides his speech, and what his lips impart increases learning" (Proverbs 16:23 NEB).
- "A wise man's tongue spreads knowledge; stupid men talk nonsense" (Proverbs 15:2 NEB).
- "When she opens her mouth, she does so wisely; on her tongue is kindly instruction" (Proverbs 31:26 JB).

Are honest

- "Honest speech is the desire of kings, they love a man who speaks the truth" (Proverbs 16:13 NEB).

- "A straightforward answer is as good as a kiss of friendship" (Proverbs 24:26 NEB).

Do not provoke arguments

- "The lips of the fool draw him into arguments and his mouth pleads for a beating" (Proverbs 18:6 JB).
- "A soft answer turns away anger, but a sharp word makes tempers hot" (Proverbs 15:1 NEB).
- "Don't have anything to do with foolish and stupid arguments, because you know they produce quarrels. And the Lord's servant must not quarrel; instead, he must be kind to everyone, able to teach, not resentful" (2 Timothy 2:23–24).

Refrain from gossip

- "A tittle-tattler lets secrets out, a trustworthy man keeps things hidden" (Proverbs 11:13 JB).
- "Gossip can be sharp as a sword, but the tongue of the wise heals" (Proverbs 12:18 NEB).
- "A scoundrel repeats evil gossip; it is like a scorching fire on his lips. Disaffection stirs up quarrels, and tale-bearing breaks up friendship" (Proverbs 16:27–28 NEB).

Use kind words to soothe and heal

- "The tongue that soothes is a tree of life; the barbed tongue, a breaker of hearts" (Proverbs 15:4 JB).
- "Kind words are like dripping honey, sweetness on the tongue and health for the body" (Proverbs 16:24 NEB).
- "Worry makes a man's heart heavy, a kindly word makes it glad" (Proverbs 12:25 JB).

Use words to encourage and build up others

- "Do not let any unwholesome talk come out of your mouths, but only what is helpful for building others up according to their needs, that it may benefit those who listen" (Ephesians 4:29).

- "Preach the Word; be prepared in season and out of season; correct, rebuke and encourage—with great patience and careful instruction" (2 Timothy 4:2).

REMEMBER OUR AUDIENCE WHEN SPEAKING AND BE GRACIOUS

- "Be wise in the way you act toward outsiders; make the most of every opportunity. Let your conversation be always full of grace, seasoned with salt, so that you may know how to answer everyone" (Colossians 4:5–6).
- "The righteous man can suit his words to the occasion; the wicked know only subversive talk" (Proverbs 10:32 NEB).
- "Always be prepared to give an answer to everyone who asks you to give the reason for the hope that you have. But do this with gentleness and respect, keeping a clear conscience, so that those who speak maliciously against your good behavior in Christ may be ashamed of their slander" (1 Peter 3:15–16).

REFRAIN FROM USING PROFANITY AND DESTRUCTIVE LANGUAGE

- "But now you must rid yourselves of all such things as these: anger, rage, malice, slander, and filthy language from your lips" (Colossians 3:8).
- "No man can tame the tongue. It is a restless evil, full of deadly poison. With the tongue we praise our Lord and Father, and with it we curse men, who have been made in God's likeness. Out of the same mouth come praise and cursing. My brothers, this should not be" (James 3:8–10).
- "Nor should there be obscenity, foolish talk or coarse joking, which are out of place, but rather thanksgiving" (Ephesians 5:4).

REFRAIN FROM NAGGING

- "A foolish son is the ruin of his father, a woman's scolding is like a dripping gutter" (Proverbs 19:13 JB).
- "Better to live in a corner of the house-top than have a nagging wife and a brawling household" (Proverbs 25:24 NEB).

It's interesting to note that in both verses above, the children's behavior is mentioned along with the woman's nagging. Children learn behaviors from observing how their parents treat one another. How we speak to our spouses lays the groundwork for how our family members speak to one another into adulthood.

First Peter 3:1–2 offers relevant insight into challenging adult relationships: "Wives, in the same way be submissive to your husbands so that, if any of them do not believe the word, they may be won over without words by the behavior of their wives, when they see the purity and reverence of your lives." These verses are sometimes misinterpreted as advising wives to submissively suffer in silence. The opposite is true. An influential wife and mother realizes that her godly behavior and example are infinitely more effective without needless words (the "dripping gutter"). The way we live impacts our families more than what we say. However, good actions can be sabotaged by careless speech.

> **CHILDREN DO NOT ALWAYS LISTEN TO THEIR PARENTS, BUT THEY NEVER FAIL TO IMITATE THEM.**
>
> JAMES BALDWIN

LISTEN FIRST AND PATIENTLY WAIT TO UNDERSTAND ANOTHER'S POSITION BEFORE SPEAKING

Remember that what we don't say is as important as what we do say. Being a good listener is critical to nurturing a healthy relationship. Analogous to music, the rests and silences are as important as the notes. The excellent advice from God's Word about engaging in discussion is to *listen first*.

- "To answer a question before you have heard it out is both stupid and insulting. A man's spirit may sustain him in sickness, but if the spirit is wounded, who can mend it? Knowledge comes to the discerning mind; the wise ear listens to get knowledge" (Proverbs 18:13–15 NEB, see also Proverbs 12:15).
- "My dear brothers, take note of this: Everyone should be quick to listen, slow to speak and slow to become angry, for man's anger does not bring about the righteous life that God desires" (James 1:19–20).

Listening before we speak requires patience, being willing to wait. Listening is different than hearing. When we listen, we make the effort to fully understand the other person's position before we comment.

Proverbs contrasts patience with anger from a sharp temper. Disputes usually arise when parties refuse to listen to one another or understand each other.

- "Bad temper provokes a quarrel, but patience heals discords" (15:18 NEB).
- "To be patient shows great understanding; quick temper is the height of folly" (14:29 NEB).
- "A stupid man gives free rein to his anger; a wise man waits and lets it grow cool" (29:11 NEB).

Patience combined with a soft tongue are the best antidotes for a sharp temper: "With patience a judge may be cajoled: a soft tongue breaks bones" (25:15 JB).

OFFER WISE COUNSEL WHEN REQUESTED BUT NOT CRIT-ICISM OR UNREQUESTED ADVICE

Criticism falls in the category of what we don't say. Criticism is constant fault-finding, which can poison a relationship. Toxic criticism can be habitual for some people. In contrast, practicing love enables us to overlook faults. Proverbs says,

- "Hate is always picking a quarrel, but love turns a blind eye to every fault" (10:12 NEB).
- "To be patient shows intelligence; to overlook faults is a man's glory" (19:11 NEB).
- "He who conceals another's offence seeks his goodwill, but he who harps on something breaks up friendship" (17:9 NEB).

The main difference between criticism and counsel is the way it is offered. Criticism is advice given though the listener doesn't request it, and is stated in a disapproving way. Counsel is sought after by the receiver with a listening ear. We offer counsel when it is requested and wanted.

Proverbs describes counsel as deep water in the well of wisdom. The listening and discerning man draws up the water. He goes looking for it.

- "Counsel in another's heart is like deep water, but a discerning man will draw it up" (20:5 NEB).
- "The words of a man's mouth are a gushing torrent, but deep is the water in the well of wisdom" (18:4 NEB).

Criticism is a gushing torrent of words from a man's mouth, while wise counsel is wisdom drawn up from the well. Criticism is overwhelming and could lead to drowning, while well water is refreshing and satisfying for a thirsty soul.

Now we realize why parents who have successful friendships with their adult children list as their number-one rule, "Never give unrequested advice." Wait until children ask and they are listening seekers. Some parents respond, "But if I have to wait for my child to ask me what I think, then I will never have the chance to share my advice." Then what does that tell you?

> **PARENTS SHOULD KEEP THEIR MOUTHS SHUT AND THEIR DOORS OPEN.**
>
> JANE ISAY

WISE WRITING

> **WRITING IS THE ART OF A LISTENING HEART.**
>
> JULIA CAMERON

While the ministry of carefully chosen spoken words is critical to becoming friends with our adult children, the written word can be even more powerful and effective. Many parents who have remained friends with their adult children credit written communication as their most valuable tool. Mothers who put fun notes in their young children's lunches or left love notes on their beds continued to send morning e-mails to their children when they moved away to college. They sent them Scripture verses, inspiring quotes, favorite song lyrics, and encouraging words. When their children were young, they established the habit of writing without expecting anything in return. Their words were gifts, and they continued to be into their child's adulthood.

Letters are most effective when they embody all the principles of wise speech. Cruel, venting letters that are written in anger to hurt, criticize, and maim the defenseless reader are toxic and should never be sent. Poisonous written words are more harmful than spoken words because they are permanent, inflicting more damage every time they are reread. Yet letters written to encourage, soothe, heal, and offer requested counsel with kind, tender words are honey for the soul. They are a gift of the heart to be savored over and over again. Both C. S. Lewis and Dietrich Bonhoeffer mentored others through their ministry of writing letters. The New Testament is filled with such letters.

Numerous verses in Scripture discuss the power of the pen. Throughout the Old Testament, God often instructs His people to write down His words as visible reminders of His guidance (Deuteronomy 6:5–9; 31:19; Ezekiel 37:20; Habakkuk 2:2–3). We are to write God's commands on the tablet of our memory (Proverbs 7:3 NEB). Peter describes the purpose of his letters as encouragement to stand fast in the truth (1 Peter 5:12) and reminders to stimulate wholesome thinking based on God's Word (2 Peter 3:1–2). One purpose of Paul's letters is to remind his readers of God's truth (Romans 15:15; Galatians 1:20). Our names are written in the book of life (Revelations 21:27) and we are inscribed on the palms of God's hands (Isaiah 49:16 NASB). The power of God's written word lies in its permanence, trustworthiness, and truth (Revelations 21:5). God's Word is living and active, sifting the purposes and thoughts of our hearts (Hebrews 4:12–13). Written words can be powerful.

> YOU YOURSELVES ARE OUR LETTER, WRITTEN ON OUR HEARTS, KNOWN AND READ BY EVERYBODY. YOU SHOW THAT YOU ARE A LETTER FROM CHRIST, THE RESULT OF OUR MINISTRY, WRITTEN NOT WITH INK BUT WITH THE SPIRIT OF THE LIVING GOD, NOT ON TABLETS OF STONE BUT ON TABLETS OF HUMAN HEARTS.
>
> 2 CORINTHIANS 3:2–3

WRITING TO HEAL

> WRITING RIGHTS THINGS.
>
> JULIA CAMERON

Written communication is a common therapy tool used with family members when verbal communication has broken down. When spouses or parents and children cannot speak to each other without erupting into heated arguments, writing letters or e-mailing can begin the healing process. Unlike spoken words, written words can be carefully chosen after much thought. They can be "heard" by the receiver when he or she chooses to listen.

Writing letters to parents is an excellent way for children to vent. My mother is a passionate person who grew up in a Latin culture where she was not allowed to express her feelings. She was severely disciplined for displaying emotion, which was considered disobedience. Aware of her pain, I decided to tell my children that they could share anything with me. They could not yell at me or be disrespectful, but they could write anything to me. When my own passionate daughter was angry, I could see the smoke coming off the pages of her letters as she wrote. After she calmed down, we read her letters and discussed her concerns. The act of writing diffused much of her anger. I have also written occasional letters to my adult children to share concerns and open a dialogue about sensitive topics. They seem to appreciate and "hear" written words more than spoken words.

PeggySue used interactive (also called dialogue) journaling with each of her growing children to give them a safe place to express their feelings without judgment. They wrote to her in their individual journals, and she wrote back to them. This format was especially helpful when feelings were too painful to discuss. When PeggySue miscarried a baby, her children grieved for their lost sibling by writing to her. When PeggySue and her husband endured a difficult divorce, their children wrote about issues they couldn't freely talk about. She continues to write to her adult children through e-mail and snail mail.

Writing to Guide and Encourage

> It is the act of writing that calls ideas forward, not ideas that call forward writing.
>
> Julia Cameron

Many families use written contracts to help their children practice being responsible and accountable, preparing them for adulthood. Some parents and children jointly write annual contracts during the child's birthday week, giving the child a new privilege as well as a new responsibility. Contracts for a young child may address getting a hamster yet requiring the child to clean the cage and feed the hamster. Driving conditions, purity abstinence contracts, decisions about refraining from drug and alcohol use, and other guidelines needed by teenagers are written in black and white, so there is no confusion about expectations, thus avoiding misunderstanding and family conflict.

It is well known that a main difference between people who regularly accomplish their goals and those who do not reach their goals is that the first group writes their goals down. Concrete, written reminders keep us on track. One family I know has an annual writing session on New Year's Eve. They write down prayers for each other. They write down their major goals for the year. Then they seal their letters in an envelope and open them the following New Year's Eve, to read before writing their new letters. They celebrate what God has done in their lives during the previous year and look forward to His guidance in the year to come.

In our family, we created journals to be read by our children as adults. Beginning with their births, my husband, their grandparents, and I wrote letters to them in a journal. We continued the practice on their birthdays, adding new letters every year. We gave each of our children their journal on their twenty-first birthday.

Our eldest daughter recently told us that she read that journal often during a challenging period in her life. She said, "When I was having a bad day, I read those letters and was reminded how much I was loved." Since some of her grandparents are now deceased, their permanent words continue to comfort and encourage her.

Tracy chronicles her writing experience with her children:

> My husband and I have always written to our children. When my children were young, I put notes in their school lunches. When they were in junior high and high school, I added educational touches. Since my daughter was studying French, I wrote her notes in French. I wrote notes to my son that included his English class vocabulary words. As a family, we wrote letters to my husband on his birthday. We created a "Birthday Book" with letters, photos, and memories of the previous year. Now that our children are grown, this book contains an annual review of our family life.
>
> Written communication became the main way we discussed serious issues with our children as teenagers. We were grateful that we had laid the groundwork of writing when we faced challenges with our teenage children. You can't argue with a letter. You have time to read it and digest it. Carefully worded letters eliminate rash words and angry reactions. When we had concerns about our children in high school, my husband or I would leave letters in their rooms for them to read when they were ready. We wrote with a positive tone, built them up, told them that we loved them, and then gently shared any

concerns. It was their choice when to respond to us but they always knew where we stood.

When our son was a college student, he began to struggle in school and we knew that he was experimenting with drugs and alcohol. My husband and I e-mailed letters to him. After our son graduated from college and started working, he told us that our letters were always helpful wake-up calls. He knew how much we loved him and wanted God's best for him. I believe that we are good friends with our adult children today because we were able to write to them and carefully choose our words to always heal, never hurt.

> **ALL WRITING IS ULTIMATELY A QUESTION OF SOLVING A PROBLEM.**
>
> WILLIAM ZINSSER

WRITING IN THE DIGITAL AGE

> **WHILE WE CALL OUR TIME THE AGE OF INFORMATION, WISDOM IS IN SHORT SUPPLY.**
>
> MARY PIPHER

While technology may have been our previous enemy to having an intimate relationship with our teenager, it now becomes our friend. When our child lived at home, we watched him or her text, chat online, and connect with friends in a myriad of electronic forms, while we longed for a face-to-face, uninterrupted conversation. Now that our children are gone, we can electronically write to them and stay in touch like any friend does. The key is to be invited.

I am a technological dinosaur who has written in books about the detrimental impact of technology on the arts, education, and family relationships. I have deep concerns about our society's screen attachment/addiction and many young persons' fast-food approach to reading and writing. I agree with Sven Birkerts, author of *The Gutenberg Elegies: The Fate of Reading in an Electronic Age*, who believes that too many young people today quickly assimilate information but have lost depth of thinking. They know facts but have not gained wisdom.

Yet when my adult children asked me to start texting with them, I immediately bought a new phone with that feature. It is the fastest way to reach each other and most convenient for them. And guess which is the fastest growing group on Facebook? Grandparents who want to stay in touch with their grandchildren comprise this group.

While I am a digital immigrant, my children are digital natives. They have grown up in an electronic culture. Since my parenting days are over, I must see the world through their eyes and connect with them in any form that nurtures our friendship—without judgment.

> MY MOTHER WAS A GREAT EXAMPLE TO ME ABOUT THE BEAUTY AND POWER OF WRITING AS A PALPABLE SIGN OF LOVE. SHE HAD SEVEN CHILDREN AND, WHEN WE WERE OFF AT SCHOOL, SHE WROTE TO US . . . MY MOTHER MAY HAVE SAID THESE THINGS OVER THE PHONE TO ME, BUT WHAT STUCK WAS THAT SHE PUT IT ON THE PAGE. SHE CARED ENOUGH TO WRITE IT.
>
> JULIA CAMERON

THE MASTER OF WISE COMMUNICATION

> IF ANYONE SPEAKS, HE SHOULD DO IT AS ONE
> SPEAKING THE VERY WORDS OF GOD.
>
> 1 PETER 4:11

Let us review Scripture's guidelines for wise communication:

1. Hold your tongue.
2. Use your words to share knowledge and increase learning.
3. Be honest.
4. Do not provoke arguments.
5. Refrain from gossip.
6. Use kind words to soothe and heal.
7. Use words to encourage and build up others.
8. Remember your audience when speaking and be gracious.
9. Refrain from using profanity and destructive language.
10. Refrain from nagging. (A godly example and gentle spirit speak much louder than unnecessary words.)
11. Listen first and patiently wait to understand another's position before speaking.
12. Offer wise counsel when requested but not criticism or unrequested advice.

It is important to realize that we are responsible only for our own words, not for our adult children's communication habits. Whether our children use words to express anger or are silent and uncommunicative, the best way we can help them practice biblical communication is to model it for them. Common sense and experience tell us that returning words spoken in anger with more angry speech or letters only escalates an altercation. Badgering a silent young person only causes him or her to retreat further from us. God gives us clear and effective guidelines for opening paths of communication to build solid relationships. Remember that they are much harder to practice than to understand.

Now let us compare the above principles of biblical communication with Jesus' approach to nurturing His disciples in chapter 2. Jesus took the time to listen to His disciples. He held His tongue, asked questions, and made an effort to understand their position before instructing them. He never became angry with the disciples or began arguments. He diffused arguments and conflicts with soft words spoken at a later time. He was always honest and open with the disciples when they asked Him questions and sought His input. He carefully chose His words to explain concepts in ways they could comprehend. Jesus did not gossip. He did not nag or criticize. Jesus did not use cruel, vulgar language. Jesus did use His words to teach, encourage, heal, and soothe. He tailored His speaking to individual audiences, making it relevant to their life experiences. Jesus Christ was the master of using wise speech in every situation He encountered. We must strive to follow His example.

WHEN YOU SPEAK, YOUR WORDS ECHO ONLY ACROSS THE ROOM OR DOWN THE HALL. BUT WHEN YOU WRITE, YOUR WORDS ECHO DOWN THE AGES.

BUD GARDNER

THE THOUGHTS CONTAINED IN A LETTER, THE KIND, UNSELFISH, PRETTY THOUGHTS OF FRIENDSHIP, REMAIN FOREVER IN THE HEART AND MIND OF THE PERSON FOR WHOM IT WAS INTENDED.

LILLIAN EICHLER

A mother shares:

My mother died when I was ten years old. My father, a pastor, did not think that he could adequately care for my brother and me so he sent us to live with our aunt. Because I know the pain of not becoming adult friends with one's parents, I was determined to have a healthy friendship with my three adult sons. My husband and I tried to nurture an environment where our children could tell us anything and know they were safe. We were also willing to apologize when we made mistakes. We've been honest about our failings to encourage them with any struggles they may face.

My husband and I made an effort to spend individual time with each of our children in addition to fun family activities and trips. We tried to find connector points with them, supporting their passions and learning about their interests. Now we are partners in ministry.

I try to stay in regular contact with my adult children through phone calls, daily e-mail messages, including Scripture encouragement, and sending packages. I look for ways to make my sons smile.

We try to respect our sons' individual journeys, especially when we would prefer they make other decisions. The key is praying for them. The less parents can say, the more they should pray. It's critical that we are good listeners, keep communication lines open, and carefully weigh our words. My aunt once said something so hurtful that it has stayed with me for a lifetime. I have prayed, "God, please stop me from saying something cruel that my sons will be unable to forget." Once words are said, they cannot be taken back.

Most important, our kids know how much we love them and enjoy them. We are always eager to rearrange our schedules if it means spending more time together.

An adult daughter shares:

I know that my mom loves me but I'm not always sure that she likes me. She certainly doesn't understand me. She enjoys spending time with my brother, but not me. I have learned to be guarded in sharing my problems with her because she will use the information to criticize me or, worse, share it with other people. She cannot listen to me without interrupting. We rarely have a conversation where she does not point out my faults. (She says that she does this to help me.) The affirming words I crave from her are absent. Then she wonders why I do not want to spend more time with her. We may be mother and daughter but we are not friends.

An adult son shares:

I did not experience an ideal childhood. My dad was abusive and my parents divorced when I was young. Yet I am good friends with my mom because she was always honest with me. Telling the truth is a good foundation for friendship.

An adult daughter shares:

I love my parents but am not close friends with them. In a friendship, two people can be completely honest with each other. My parents divorced while I was planning my wedding. In the midst of discussing wedding invitations and centerpieces, I knew my parents were discussing divorce proceedings. My siblings and I have not been able to get a straight, honest answer about why they divorced.

Any time spent with either parent is stressful because I always have to watch what I say. I learned during my teen years that whatever my siblings and I say can come back to hurt us.

After the divorce, my dad started dating and soon was engaged to his girlfriend. My siblings and I have not been included in his new relationship.

I do work at a relationship with both parents. I love spending time with my family. I've learned to keep the peace and avoid the hurt. But my priority is to work on my own marriage now.

Life is the first gift, love is the second, and understanding the third.

Margie Piercy

Oh, the comfort—the inexpressible comfort, of feeling safe with a person—having neither to weigh thoughts nor measure words, but pouring them all right out, just as they are chaff and grain together; certain that a faithful hand will take and sift them, keep what is worth keeping and then, with the breath of kindness, blow the rest away.

Dinah Craik

Seeing one's parents as people, as individuals outside of their parental roles, is one of the more advanced markers of the transition to adulthood.

Hara Marano

FIVE

TREATING OUR CHILDREN
AS FRIENDS

THE ONLY WAY TO HAVE A FRIEND IS TO BE
ONE.

RALPH WALDO EMERSON

Michael was always his parents' favorite child, his mother's pampered, only son. As Michael grew up, he had problems with his temper, addictions, failed marriages, and financial and legal problems. His sisters watched their parents dote on Michael and bail him out of his endless difficulties. They did not receive the same attention or resources.

Michael and his parents were inseparable but they were not friends. Michael was not friends with his sisters and his sisters were not friends with their parents. Michael's parents crippled him and alienated their daughters. It is not a coincidence that Michael's sisters became capable, independent women. Their parents did not bail out their daughters so they learned to be responsible people. Michael's parents did him no favors.

Healthy friendships with our adult children are close relationships but not all close relationships with adult children are healthy friendships. Some parents feel unusually connected to their children, telling friends, "We have always been so close." A twenty-eight-year-old woman who has always been Daddy's Little Princess and is still bankrolled for everything her heart desires may feel close to her father, but they are not friends. A mother who continues to micromanage her adult daughter's life, calls and texts throughout the day, and acts as her personal life assistant feels involved in her daughter's daily life, but they are not friends. Anthony is a thirty-five-year-old man who lives with his mother. She still takes care of him and he has become her companion. They have an enmeshed, dependent relationship but do not enjoy a healthy friendship.

BEST OF BOTH WORLDS

> TRUE FRIENDSHIPS ARE CHARACTERIZED BY GRACE, TRUTH, FORGIVENESS, UNSELFISHNESS, BOUNDARIES, CARE, AND LOVE IN GIGANTIC AND MUTUAL PROPORTION.
>
> LUCI SWINDOLL

Think of your closest, healthiest friendships. With your closest friends, I would imagine that you initiate and enjoy spending time together, feel the freedom to tell each other anything without judgment, support one another's dreams and passions, play together and attend special events to cheer them on, laugh together, see their heart and appreciate their unique qualities, keep their confidences and defend them when others criticize them, pray for them, unconditionally love them, are honest with them, respect them and receive respect, understand that they may respond to God in different ways than you do, and carefully choose your words when communicating.

With the exception of specific parental tasks, such as protection and letting go, these are the foundation blocks for a good relationship with your adult child. This entire book can be summarized in one statement: *The key to having great friendships with your adult children is to treat them as you would treat any close friend.* Whenever you are unsure of your words or actions, stop and ask

yourself, "Would I say or do this with my close friend, _____?"
If we treat a twenty-six-year-old man like a young child, he will
probably act like a child. If we treat him like a mature adult friend,
he will probably rise to our expectations.

When we treat our children as friends, we are not treating
them as distant acquaintances. Do not misinterpret the suggestion
to treat your child as a friend as instruction to be silent or uninvolved. Our children become some of our closest friends. We balance this with the knowledge that the mother/father role always
trumps the friend role. We have only one mother and one father,
while we have several close friends. There are no substitutes for
the people who birthed and raised us.

We are not seeking to be our child's best friend in their peer
group, just as we would not want our child to take the place of
our closest peer friend. Yet if your close friends were in crisis,
wouldn't you drop everything and run to help them? If your
close friends were hospitalized, in the midst of a divorce, recently
fired, or dealing with tragic loss, wouldn't you be there to walk
through the pain with them? Wouldn't you open your home,
help with child care, offer them meals, and do whatever you
could to ease their pain? If your close friend was about to jump
off a cliff (e.g., leave her husband and three children to have an
affair with her boss), would you remain silent or warn her of the
consequences? Close friends speak up and take action in legitimate crises.

A mom or dad can be the best of both worlds, a close friend
and caring parent for a lifetime. When their daughter, Tanya,
became ill with an aggressive cancer, Marcia and Daniel put their
lives on hold to take care of their daughter and help with their
grandchildren's care. They made it possible for Tanya's husband to
visit her in the hospital without worrying about their kids. Tanya's
close friends from her church community also brought meals to
the home, helped drive Tanya to chemotherapy treatments and her
children to school, and rallied around the family.

Parents have the privilege of being a loving safety net in legitimate crises. But the test of a healthy friendship with one's adult children comes in day-to-day life, absent of crisis. For example, if your close friend was behind on her bills because of credit card debt, would you pay her bills? If you have a healthy friendship, you would lend a supportive ear, but you would not pay her bills. Would you call your friend in the morning to make sure he had awakened in time to be at an important appointment? No, that would be insulting. When we rescue adults, we communicate that we have no confidence in them. Rescuing our adult children communicates the same message. If your close friend disagreed with you and did not follow your suggestions for solving her problems, would you become angry and stop talking to her?

You probably wouldn't leave this phone message for your close friend: "Why haven't you called me? I haven't heard from you in a while." Can you imagine greeting your closest friend with, "Your hair looks awful. And that's not a good color on you. Have you gained weight?" Do you comment on your friend's housekeeping skills if her home looks less than pristine?

When your friends share their problems with you, do you immediately tell them what to do or do you patiently listen, and then ask, "How can I help?" When you have lunch or coffee with your friends, I doubt that you drill them with questions to make sure that their lives are on track. When your friends experience struggles, I doubt that you are concerned about how their problems reflect on you and your influence. With friends, we cheer on their dreams but don't fund them. We encourage them to embrace their passions but don't enable irresponsible behavior. We need to treat our adult children as we would want to be treated by any adult friend.

MUTUAL RESPECT

THE PUREST FORM OF LOVE IS UNCONDITIONAL. FRIENDSHIP IS A PRECIOUS GIFT, BUT RESPECT AND TRUST ARE ALWAYS EARNED.

Mutual respect is a sign of healthy adult friendship. For example, my adult children always voluntarily call to let my husband and me know that they are safe when they travel. They also expect us to do the same. If we forget to call them, they call to check on us. Their dad traveled for a living while they were growing up and called nightly to let us know that he was safe. Our children learned that expecting to know that a family member is safe is not a parent-child issue of control, but a loving gesture between caring adults. Now, as our friendship with our children grows, we treat each other with the same respect and concern. We are nurturing a mutual, equitable relationship between adults. Sometimes they ask for our input and advice. Since they are professionals in their respective fields, we ask them for advice and seek out their expertise too.

We respect our friends' time and schedules. When planning family events, we should ask what days and times are convenient for our children and plan accordingly. We would never plan a dinner with friends by first setting the best date for us. We would tell our friends that we would love to see them and then ask what date would be most convenient for them. When close friends call after being out of touch for a while, we don't chastise them for not calling sooner, but are thrilled to hear from them and catch up.

Good friends understand each other and respect one another's different preferences and temperaments. We know which friends are introverts or extroverts, those who enjoy one-on-one time or a gregarious event. We know which friends are verbal processors or private, internal processors. Depending on our friends' busy schedules, we know which friends prefer to connect through phone conversations, texting, e-mail, video chat, or a lunch break during the work day. Connecting with our children is no different.

As parents, we should have the advantage of knowing our children's natural bent better than anyone, since we've observed our sons and daughters since birth. We become friends when we respect those differences and respond with understanding and compassion. When one of my daughters is upset, the more she can talk about it, the better she feels. Venting is helpful for her. The more pain that my other daughter is in, the less she can talk about it. She hibernates. When I haven't heard from one child for a week, I know that she is busy and doing well, with no major crises. With another, I realize that she may be having a rough time and look for ways to connect and pamper her. My son does not enjoy phone conversations, texting, or e-mailing. But he tells me, "Do keep sending those care packages."

There is no set formula for relating to our children. The way we connect to them as adults is as varied as the people they are. Our job is to pay close attention. For example, I have always tried to write thank-you notes to my children for gifts or acts of kindness, just as I would write to any friend. Too often children are expected to send thank-you notes but rarely receive them. If engrossed in conversation with my children, I do not interrupt to answer the phone, just as I would respect time with any friend. Our children learn how to treat us and others by observing how we treat our friends and them.

Treating our independent adult children like guests when they visit is one of our most enjoyable parental privileges. We make their favorite foods, block out our schedule to spend time with them, plan special activities they enjoy, and offer them a relaxing retreat from the stress of their lives. Whether they visit for an afternoon or a week, we want to give them a refreshing mini-vacation. Our home will always be their home. Our children can drop in any time and we are thrilled to see them. Most adult children have keys to their parents' homes, even if their parents move. We will always be considered parents and caretakers. Yet to have a great relationship with one's children, we understand that the reverse is not necessarily true. We do not have the freedom to drop in any time uninvited. We do not ask for keys to their homes, though we can accept them if offered. We are respectful friends and guests. The double standard may seem odd, but it works well for many families.

The key to friendship is to consistently treat our children with the same kindness, respect, thoughtfulness, and hospitality that we would offer to any friend. Raising self-sufficient adult children affords us the delightful privilege of pampering and hosting them in appropriate ways. If you took your good friend out for a birthday lunch, imagine how shocked you would be if that same friend then asked you for a loan to pay bills. Independent children observe those same boundaries.

SPIRITUAL PEERS

> **THERE IS ALWAYS AN INTANGIBLE SOMETHING WHICH MAKES A FRIEND; IT IS NOT WHAT HE DOES BUT WHAT HE IS.**
>
> OSWALD CHAMBERS

Just as important as treating our children as friends is treating them as equals in God's sight. We are spiritual peers. We may be a little farther down the road, but we are on the same journey. Our job is to encourage them to follow God's voice. Throughout Scripture, God often called young people to depart from a set path to follow Him. Realize that your children's God-given gifts and calling may be different than yours or radically different than what you envisioned for their future. Many spouses have learned that the key to an enduring marriage is treating one another as one would treat a close friend, with an abundance of compassion, grace, mercy, unconditional love, gentleness, understanding, respect, and kindness. On spiritual issues, where we have legitimate biblical concerns, we know how ineffective it is for one spouse to try to be the other spouse's "holy spirit." We want to encourage our children to listen to God instead of trying to move them in the direction we think they should go.

Sometimes our children inspire us to listen more carefully to God's whispers when we have become entrenched in our ways.

God can speak to us through our children. When Toni was recovering from a painful divorce, causing her career and finances to suffer, her adult daughter regularly encouraged her to focus on the future. Her daughter also paid for Toni to attend a professional conference to reignite her career passion and develop new networking opportunities. Toni had always been her daughter's life cheerleader. Now Toni's daughter cheered her mother on.

One mark of adulthood is for children to view parents as human beings apart from their parental roles, understanding their regrets and problems. Burdening children with our problems can be destructive during their formative years, yet honestly sharing mistakes and insights as spiritual peers can strengthen adult friendship between parents and children. Knowing the truth leads to understanding, which is the key to compassion between friends.

We are the links in God's chain of compassion. When we treat our children as adult friends and spiritual peers, we can pass on the comfort we receive from God and, in turn, receive it from them.

PRAISE BE TO THE GOD AND FATHER OF OUR LORD JESUS CHRIST, THE FATHER OF COMPASSION AND THE GOD OF ALL COMFORT, WHO COMFORTS US IN ALL OUR TROUBLES, SO THAT WE CAN COMFORT THOSE IN ANY TROUBLE WITH THE COMFORT WE OURSELVES HAVE RECEIVED FROM GOD.

2 CORINTHIANS 1:3–5

A mother shares:

My daughters, husband, and I agree that the main reason we are close friends is that we have practiced being connected. When our daughters were in college, I sent them an e-mail greeting every morning. Now that my daughters are married and working in careers, our younger daughter regularly calls us on her way home from work. We see our older daughter often because we help care for her young child.

Our daughters watched us be equally connected to our parents and extended family. We have been protective of family time, instilling in our children that family comes first. When our children were young, we protected family vacations and holiday celebrations. Now that our daughters have their own families, we have to be creative planners. We tailor activities around their interests and schedules. For example, when our eldest daughter and her husband took up snowshoeing and invited us on an excursion, we learned to snowshoe.

We enjoy treating our daughters and sons-in-law to dinner, whether we meet at their favorite restaurant or bring a meal to their home. We enjoy playing games together. We go to them instead of asking them to come to us, making it more convenient for our children. We extend frequent invitations but never make them feel guilty for declining. My husband has invested in developing individual friendships with his sons-in-law, even taking them on road trips.

I watched some of my friends sabotage their relationships with their children when they didn't agree with their choices or didn't approve of their spouses. My husband and I made a conscious decision to watch our words and keep focused on building relationships.

Our most significant challenge was the first Christmas that our daughters and their families traveled to visit their in-laws. We decided to host them for a foreign-themed celebration the week before Christmas. We had so much fun that our children asked to make it an annual event, celebrating "Christmas in a different country" each year. It is never too late to start new family traditions.

An adult daughter shares:

Growing up in a strong Christian home, I never expected my parents to divorce. The sad truth is that Christian parents get divorced. Trying to maintain a good adult relationship with my parents is challenging. It's a balancing act, not a friendship. Major holidays are especially stressful. They have become painful reminders that my parents' marriage is no longer intact. Since both my parents moved after their divorce, my siblings and I do not have a family home filled with memories to gather in. Instead of looking forward to returning home, we dread having to negotiate complicated schedules in order to carve out time with each parent. Since our parents continue to harbor bitterness toward each other, we are caught in the middle and pay the price. Adult children are just as affected by their parents' divorce as young children.

An adult daughter shares:

I think that I am good friends with my parents because I never felt responsible for them or my siblings. Our job as young adults is to become responsible for ourselves, which is almost impossible if we feel responsible for our parents' well-being. As the eldest child in my family, my parents guarded me from becoming a second parent to my siblings.

My parents gave me the freedom to make choices without any guilt. We respect and trust each other. They have confidence in me. We can be honest and direct. I never have to worry that my parents are saying one thing but actually thinking another. We have clear communication. They always listen to me and are consistently there for me but don't make a habit of telling me what to do. They know

I will figure it out. My parents are a great sounding board when I'm making decisions.

My family has a strong identity at its core but it's flexible, not rigid. Our relationships have evolved and changed over the years. When asked if I was good friends with my parents, I realized that I had never actually thought about it. I simply like going home and hanging out with my parents and siblings. I would choose them to be friends. The relationships feel safe, effortless, and natural. I believe that it's the parent's job to make that transition to friendship easy, not the child's job.

A mother is a woman who has taken on an extra life . . . she'll be two people in one skin for the rest of her days.

Pam Brown

What is a friend? A single soul dwelling in two bodies.

Aristotle

I know I would be doing you the greatest disservice of all to deprive you of life's own education. If birds didn't push their awkward offspring from the nest and force them to flap and flutter to keep from slamming to the ground, the babies would grow fat and immobile in the nest. When it came time to migrate, they would be left behind. Protected from the danger of early flight, they would have been sentenced to die from inertia.

Jerry Jenkins, *As You Leave Home: Parting Thoughts from a Loving Parent*

SIX

LETTING GO COMPLETELY

A MOTHER IS NOT A PERSON TO LEAN ON BUT
A PERSON TO MAKE LEANING UNNECESSARY.
DOROTHY CANFIELD FISHER

Now we come to the most challenging task in becoming friends with our adult children: separating and letting go of them completely. We must live out the well-loved analogy of having to let go of one trapeze to reach for the next one swinging toward us. It is impossible to tightly hold on to our children and become adult friends. We cannot hold two trapeze bars swinging in opposite directions. Sometimes as children try to separate, parents hold on tighter in an attempt to remain close. However, cleanly separating from children is the only way we can become adult friends with them. This can be the most difficult, painful step for parents who have been intimately involved in the details of their children's lives for two decades.

I wrote *When You're Facing the Empty Nest: Avoiding Midlife Meltdown When Your Child Leaves Home* to cope with the departure of my oldest child. Writing has always been the most effective way for me to process my pain, and interviewing other parents about their journeys comforted me that I was not alone in my grief. When I asked one friend to describe her experience when her children left home, she answered, "Oh, that's easy. When one of my children leaves home, it's like having another limb cut off."

Because my husband traveled weekly for his job, my children were my companions. We had easy, enjoyable relationships. Amputation sounded extreme . . . until I experienced it.

I thought I was a veteran after my two daughters left to attend college in different parts of our state and then settled into their careers. But the worst was yet to come, when my son—my youngest child—decided to attend college three thousand miles away on the opposite coast. My house was silent. As parents of sons know, we rarely heard from him. My son and I had been unusually close so I was unprepared for the swift and clean amputation. Then I realized the truth that I had observed in others' lives but, of course, thought wouldn't happen to me. The closer a mother is to her son, the more he needs to sever the cord to become a man. Genesis 2:24 states that a man shall leave his father and mother. Most women embrace that verse when it applies to their husbands separating from their mothers to cleave to their wives but it is a tougher pill to swallow when it applies to their own sons.

As I talked to more mothers of young adult sons, I realized that the altered mother-son relationship is normal and healthy. Veteran mothers have told me that communication improved as their sons matured once the cord was firmly cut. Now when I encounter a mother who is mourning the loss of a close relationship with her son who has recently left home, I want to say, "Congratulations. This means that you have done your parenting job well. You have raised a man." We mothers are in good company, which I learned when I read the Gospels through a mother's eyes, observing Jesus' relationship with His mother, Mary.

JESUS AS MARY'S SON

Jesus was the perfect son of God, yet He was not an ideal earthly son. He was fully human. View His childhood through a parent's eyes. Can you imagine driving home from church to realize that one of your children is missing? You search for your son everywhere and do not find him for days. Mary and

Joseph experience this in Luke 2:41–52. Jesus remained in Jerusalem after his parents left. I think He must have purposefully evaded them. Mary and Joseph return to the city and look for Him everywhere. When they find Him after three days, Mary confronts Jesus, "Son, why have you treated us like this? Your father and I have been anxiously searching for you." Jesus does not apologize and answers their questions with His questions, "Why were you searching for me? Didn't you know I had to be in my Father's house?" Then He returns to Nazareth with His parents and is obedient to them, and grows "in wisdom and stature, and in favor with God and men."

We remember Jesus' first miracle of turning water into wine at the wedding at Cana in Galilee, but let's view it through a mother's eyes (John 2:1–11). Mary told Jesus, "They have no more wine." Jesus replied, "Why do you involve me? My time has not yet come." Does this sound familiar? Can't you hear our own sons' replies when we ask them for help: "Why are you bothering me now?" Still Mary tells the servants, "Do whatever he tells you," and Jesus supplies more wine for the wedding.

As Jesus' ministry begins, His family thinks He is out of his mind and tries to take charge of Him (Mark 3:21). Jesus is in a home with His disciples, speaking to the crowd. His mother and brothers arrive and send someone to get Him.

> A crowd was sitting around him, and they told him, "Your mother and brothers are outside looking for you." "Who are my mother and my brothers?" he asked. Then he looked at those seated in a circle around him and said, "Here are my mother and my brothers! Whoever does God's will is my brother and sister and mother." (Mark 3:32–35)

Jesus ignores His family, including His mother, and does not come outside.

In Luke 11:27–28, when the woman calls out, "Blessed is the mother who gave you birth and nursed you," Jesus does not acknowledge His mother's care or give her any credit. He focuses on His message: "Blessed rather are those who hear the word of God and obey it." As a mother, I don't understand why Jesus could not respond, "Yes, my mother is wonderful and caring, but more blessed are those who hear the word of God and obey it." What would have been so wrong with also honoring the mother who raised Him?

In these instances, Jesus is sharing great theological truth with His followers, but He is also cutting the cord. He must cut the cord with His mother to follow God's purpose for His life. When Simeon blessed baby Jesus in the temple, Simeon told Mary:

> This child is destined to cause the falling and rising of many in Israel, and to be a sign that will be spoken against, so that the thoughts of many hearts will be revealed. And a sword will pierce your own soul too. (Luke 2:34–35)

Prior to Simeon's prophecy, Mary had no idea what God had called her son to do. Neither did she know how painful it would be for her to watch Him suffer. Simeon's words are a different message than the one Mary received from the angel, Gabriel, about her son in the womb: "He will be great and will be called the Son of the Most High. The Lord God will give him the throne of his father David, and he will reign over the house of Jacob forever; his kingdom will never end" (Luke 1:32–33).

God gives Mary a clear vision of His *purpose* for Jesus, but He does not tell Mary how that will be accomplished. Mary trusts God, even though she does not understand how "a sword will pierce [her] own soul too." We mothers can relate to Mary's journey. We trust that God's hand is on our children's lives and He will lead them in His purposes. Yet often we are unprepared for the path God will lead them on. Our souls can be pierced too. We didn't anticipate the pain. Experiencing "cord cutting" can be painful, but the step is necessary in order for our children to follow God's purpose for their lives. Even Jesus had to sever the cord with His mother and family to follow God's purpose for His life.

Often in our own lives, God shows us the final biblical goal or result (e.g., become the mirror of Jesus Christ), but He does not attach a complete list of steps to reach it. Nor does God ask for our input or permission about the path He chooses for us or our children. Gordon Smith says, "A simple rule of thumb: God only leads us one step at a time."[1] This is the meat of trust and faith.

WE ARE STEWARDS

> WHOEVER SAID IT FIRST SPOKE WITH INSIGHT AND WISDOM; YOU DON'T OWN CHILDREN, YOU ONLY BORROW THEM.
>
> ANNE LINN

Of all parents, followers of Jesus Christ should be the most comfortable with letting go of their children, yet sometimes we are the worst examples of helicopter parents. We should know that we can't control their lives or hone them into perfect products. We don't control our own lives. Further, God does not call us to live sanitized, protected lives. An ideal, happy life is never the goal for a follower of Jesus Christ. Our goal is to teach our children to trust God and follow Him.

As Christians, we should not worship our children or put them in the place of our salvation or life purpose. God alone deserves our worship. Phrases like "family first" and "our children always come first" are used and accepted, even respected, in our culture, outside and inside the church. Parents often consider their children as their top priority when making decisions. It's sobering to realize that this approach may not be in a child's best interest.

We Christian parents should understand that our adult children were on loan to us when they were younger. Read chapters 1 and 2 of 1 Samuel to relive Hannah's deep heartache of infertility; her joy at receiving the gift of her son, Samuel, from God; and her second deep heartache as she returns Samuel back to God after he is weaned. Hannah offers a prayer of praise to God as she leaves her son with Eli the priest (2:1–10). Every mother understands Hannah's grief as she praises and declares who God is in the midst of her pain. This is ultimate trust. Hannah will visit Samuel only once a year: "Every year his mother made him a little cloak and took it to him when she went up with her husband to offer the annual sacrifice" (1 Samuel 2:19 NEB). Hannah will have five more children, yet they do not take the place of her firstborn son, the infant she desperately longed to hold.

We too have been stewards of children who belong to God, though we may keep them in our homes several years longer than Hannah did. We enjoyed the privilege, not the right, of taking care of them as they made their way to adulthood. Our first job was to ferociously protect our children. Our last job is to get out of God's way. He is the ultimate parent who guides their every step.

TAKING A STAND

> NURTURING SOMETIMES HAS TO ASSUME THE
> FORM OF NOT GIVING.
>
> AARON AUERBACH

Parents of capable, independent adults of the Millennial generation at some point took a stand. These parents let go and expected their children to become the independent adults they are today. When presented with their child's various problems, these parents usually responded, "You're smart. Go figure it out." To their children, their parents' behavior seemed almost cruel at times, when their friends were living at home rent-free with no responsibilities.

The parents who encouraged independence never bailed their children out of problems, especially financial ones. Whether their children received a speeding ticket or left a school project at home on the day it was due, these parents did not come to the rescue. They wouldn't think of meddling in their child's school or work problem by talking to a teacher or boss. They often began the weaning process in high school, encouraging their children to find summer jobs to contribute to their expenses. If they wanted a car, these "adults in process" contributed to gas and auto insurance. When these children attended college, they found part-time or summer work to pay for their books or provide their own spending money. They learned to be contributing adults. In one family, the parents refused to be their children's personal assistants once they entered high school. Their children made their own appointments and kept them, communicated with teachers and coaches, and were fully responsible for their day-to-day activities.

Most parents with self-sufficient adult children communicated clear expectations. One dad explains:

> My parents were always tough on me, teaching me to work hard and be productive. I wanted to pass that on to my kids. I made two things clear when they left for college. It wouldn't be fair to surprise them midstream. First, I would pay for four years of college, no more. If they delayed graduation, they would fund it. All of my children graduated in four years. Second, they were always welcome to visit but not live at home. They needed to be financially independent. One of my daughters wanted to pursue the arts. My wife and I have cheered her on all the way but made it clear that we wouldn't fund it. She worked nights and weekends to support herself while going to auditions and attending graduate

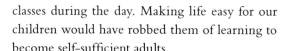

classes during the day. Making life easy for our children would have robbed them of learning to become self-sufficient adults.

This dad may seem unusually tough but he has always been an exceptionally fun dad, constantly playing with his children. He was able to separate his playful relationship with them from his high expectations. His children respect him. His daughter told me, "We learned to play hard from my dad but we also learned by watching him that hard work made the fun times possible. I grew up observing that balance. When I am at the office, I work hard, but when I am at home or on vacation, I play hard with my family and friends."

BOOMERANG CHILDREN

> MOVING BACK HOME CAN BE A REDEEMING EXPERIENCE IF IT DOESN'T LAST ANY LONGER THAN NECESSARY. OUR FAMILY OFFERS US A HAVEN WHEN NO ONE ELSE WILL, THEY OFFER US A PLACE OF REFUGE AND RECOVERY WHEN WE HAVE NOWHERE ELSE TO TURN. FAMILY CAN TURN OUT TO BE FRIENDS, AS DEFINED BY JESUS' STANDARD: "I WAS HUNGRY AND YOU GAVE ME SOMETHING TO EAT, I WAS THIRSTY AND YOU GAVE ME SOMETHING TO DRINK, I WAS A STRANGER AND YOU INVITED ME IN, I NEEDED CLOTHES AND YOU CLOTHED ME, I WAS SICK AND YOU LOOKED AFTER ME."
>
> RICHARD NELSON BOLLES

Boomerang children, young adults who return to the family home to live, can pose the greatest challenge to adult friendship.

Some children in their twenties return home immediately after college while others in their forties may return with children after a divorce or job loss. Parents who enjoy healthy adult friendships with their children usually discouraged them from moving home after their career preparation (college, apprenticeships, or other training programs). The message was, "Once you leave, don't come back." In light of our current economic situation, this stand may not be as realistic today.

I have come to the conclusion that the key is not *if* children return to live at home but *how* they live at home. Some parents require monthly rent from their children. Some use the money for necessary home expenses, while others put the rent money in a savings account for their children. Before allowing adult children to move home, we must ask ourselves: Will living at home cripple our children or lead to self-sufficient adulthood? Does living at home serve a constructive purpose? In some cultures, adult children are expected to live at home with their extended family.

Amy lives at home and works full-time, contributing to her family's expenses and mortgage payment. She helps to care for older relatives who also live in the family home. Lisa lives at home while pursuing her teaching credentials and working as an unpaid student teacher. Daniel lives at home because he lost his job due to the recession. He continues to look for work but also helps with the youth ministry in his church and volunteers at a homeless shelter. Amy, Lisa, and Daniel are each contributing to their futures, families, or communities. Living at home may be helping them to reach a self-sufficient, productive adulthood. Joshua lives at home with no responsibilities, does not work or attend school, does not pay rent or help with his family's expenses, and expects his family to take care of him. Living at home is denying Joshua the opportunity to become an independent adult. In biblical terms, Joshua has settled into a lifestyle of idleness.

The Scriptures direct us to guard against idleness. Numerous verses in Proverbs and Paul's letters caution us that idleness leads to self-destruction. If we are healthy adults, we should work, not only to support ourselves, but to provide for others in need (Ephesians 4:28). We are called to be an example, not a burden (1 Thessalonians 4:11–12; 2 Thessalonians 3:6–10).

Some parents make the difficult, complicated decision to raise their grandchildren when their own children are unable to be responsible parents. They do not want to enable their children, but they also do not want their grandchildren to pay the price for their parents' problems. Those of us who have not walked in their shoes should not question or judge their choices.

In talking to parents and children, I have been struck by the different paths they take to becoming adult friends. Just as there is no precise formula for raising a child, there is no one-size-fits-all formula for reaching adult friendship. Lisa told me that her daughter started to cut the cord in junior high school. After graduating from high school, she moved out and never returned to live at home. Her parents respected their daughter's path, completely let go, and today they are close adult friends. In contrast, Tim decided to move home when his father who suffered with dementia became ill with cancer. Tim helped to care for his father through his death and supported his mother through her grief. He also helped her with maintenance projects in their family home. Tim and his parents became close adult friends. Living at home is rarely the issue. Mutual respect and contribution are the necessary ingredients for a healthy adult friendship.

Parents must also be brutally honest with themselves. I selfishly would have loved for my children to move back home after college. Their companionship is a great comfort to me. My husband deserves all the credit for guiding our children to become independent, because he made it clear that returning home was not an option. He regularly told me, "Ships are safe in the harbor but that's not what ships are for." Tangibly letting go has been my final, and most painful, gift of love and sacrifice to my children. Treating my children as adults marks a new journey.

GETTING OUT OF GOD'S WAY

> EACH TRANSITION WILL INVOLVE SOME KIND OF
> LOSS. GROWTH WILL ALWAYS BE COSTLY; A NEW
> VENTURE WILL ALWAYS INVOLVE SOME FORM OF
> LETTING GO.
>
> GORDON SMITH

When we are physically injured or recovering from surgery, we are often sent to work with a physical therapist. Our sessions are painful, as the therapist stretches us and exercises our bodies. If we remain immobilized and comfortable, we will never heal. We will permanently lose our range of motion. Being stretched and challenged by a physical therapist results in independent movement. The road to independence and healing is painful, whether it involves an injured shoulder or a maturing adult child, but it is necessary.

I work with special needs students, and I have observed that as they approach adulthood, their parents work harder at making them independent. Independence is the parents' main goal, and they teach their children to persevere through limitations. They stretch and push their children to their limits. Some of my special needs students have graduated from college and received teaching credentials. Ironically, some gifted, bright students who have been micromanaged by their parents are unable to function as independently as my former students. They are protected, not stretched or challenged.

Parents who raise independent children know this important biblical fact: Pain and discomfort are not our enemies. Earthly happiness is never the goal. Growth in Jesus Christ is the goal. John Henry Jowett says, "God comforts us not to make us comfortable but to make us comforters." God's goal for our children and us is to daily become more like Jesus Christ. We want our children to spiritually and personally flourish. In order for our children to have passionate, intimate relationships with God and follow Him with all of their hearts, we need to get out of God's way.

We also need to align our vision with God's vision. When I ask parents what they want for their children's future, they often respond, "Oh, I just want them to be happy." That may be the typical, acceptable answer but it is not a biblical goal, as Dr. Linda Wagener and Dr. Richard Beaton explain:

> There is an important distinction between happiness and flourishing. Happiness, or at least the capacity to experience it regularly, is a partial measure of well-being, but it is a relatively shallow measure. Shallow, because happiness can be a fleeting emotion that is dependent upon a life free of pain, adversity, or even boredom. Adversity and challenge are important ingredients in the development of a quality human being. Thus, using resources to ensure happiness and avoid pain can short-circuit the development of important elements in a flourishing life. Qualities such as resilience and empathy are the result of adversity and pain. A familiar example may help illustrate this. We accept that we need to give our children immunizations throughout their childhood in spite of the fact that shots hurt. We recognize that their bodies need to combat the virus in a weak form in order to build the capacity to resist the disease in its virulent form. Likewise, in life, we need adversity and challenge to build our capacities, engage our creativity, develop our compassion and motivate our forward movement. When all are able to flourish, we will feel that we have indeed glorified God with our humanity.[2]

Our job as parents is to immunize our children so they will flourish as adults. Like Hannah, we raise and nurture them to give them to the Lord to use for their lifetimes. Then we lean on God our Rock and, through our tears, praise Him.

AFTER THE SACRIFICE THEY TOOK THE CHILD TO ELI. "SIR, DO YOU REMEMBER ME?" HANNAH ASKED HIM. "I AM THE WOMAN WHO STOOD HERE THAT TIME PRAYING TO THE LORD! I ASKED HIM TO GIVE ME THIS CHILD, AND HE HAS GIVEN ME MY REQUEST; AND NOW I AM GIVING HIM TO THE LORD FOR AS LONG AS HE LIVES." SO SHE LEFT HIM THERE AT THE TABERNACLE FOR THE LORD TO USE. THIS WAS HANNAH'S PRAYER: "HOW I REJOICE IN THE LORD! HOW HE HAS BLESSED ME! NOW I HAVE AN ANSWER FOR MY ENEMIES, FOR THE LORD HAS SOLVED MY PROBLEM. HOW I REJOICE! NO ONE IS AS HOLY AS THE LORD! THERE IS NO OTHER GOD, NOR ANY ROCK LIKE OUR GOD."

1 SAMUEL 1:25–2:2 THE LIVING BIBLE

A father shares:

I love being the father of adult children. I no longer need to raise them. That 24/7 job is finished. I can cheer them on from the stands. I can be president of their fan club. I can be a trusted advisor and mentor them in pursuing their passions and careers. I was inspired to let go of my children by hearing Howard Hendricks speak at a conference over thirty years ago. He made such an impression on me as a young adult that I never forgot his advice.

Howard Hendricks said that parents need to stay focused on raising adults, not children. For example, parents pick up and move young children when they don't like what they are doing but that approach doesn't work with teenagers. The older children become, the less parents should be intervening. The goal of raising children is for them to require zero intervention as they reach adulthood.

My wife may have mixed feelings as our children move to other states to pursue their ministries and careers, but I say, "Fly from the nest. Soar as high as you can. My job is completed."

An adult daughter shares:

I am in my late twenties and admit that I am a full member of the entitlement generation. My parents were very supportive, always telling me how loved and special I was, that I could accomplish any-thing, and to aim for my dreams. My generation thinks that happi-ness is a right, not a privilege. Our battle cry is, "Never settle. Don't sacrifice your dreams," which our parents encouraged. My wake-up call came after I graduated from college and my parents reminded me that they would still cheer me on but they wouldn't fund the pursuit of my dream. Happiness is not a right. It's also not a biblical goal.

I've come to the conclusion that many of my friends, in their determination to "not settle," have only settled in a different way. They are entering their thirties still looking for the dream job and perfect spouse. My generation seems to be comfortable waiting in limbo for our big chance at happiness. Yet what if that moment never comes?

A mother shares:

I have always told my daughters that the best predictor of how a potential husband will treat them later in life is how he treats his mother today. Courting and honeymoon seasons can be deceiving because a couple is on its best behavior. The way a daughter relates to her dad is also a great indicator of how she will someday relate to her husband. As parents, we have a tremendous responsibility to cultivate healthy future relationships in the soil of our children's lives. We are preparing them to bond with their future mates and children.

As a mom, I enjoyed a close, peaceful, and enjoyable relationship with my son. When he went far away to college, he easily transferred this bond to a young woman who became his girlfriend and future spouse. I had to completely step back and recede from his life. This step was absolutely necessary to his manhood and painful for me. Any dad or mom who enjoys a special bond with his or her children knows how tough this experience can be. We tell ourselves, "This is healthy. This means I have done my job well," but it is tough to completely let go without feeling replaced.

Parents can only give good advice or put them on the right paths, but the final forming of a person's character lies in their own hands.

Anne Frank

Here's our dirty little secret—a lot of us are disappointed in our adult children. In the ones who still haven't lived up to their potential, whose lives seem to have come to a full stop just when they ought to be starting, or who've dead-ended down dark or dangerous alleys. And we're not only disappointed—we're ashamed of feeling that way.

Jane Adams

The product appears to be incomplete. Like a cabinet with wobbly doors, squeaky hinges, and a rough, uneven finish, it needs more work—a lot more work. But the time comes when we have no choice. The product is leaving whether we think it's ready or not. The parent must say to himself, this child is no longer in my hands. The good news is that God will travel with our son or daughter. They won't be going alone. This is the true hope of every believing parent.

Bill Coleman

SEVEN

BEING A FRIEND WHEN WE DON'T AGREE WITH OUR CHILDREN'S CHOICES

BUT WHILE HE WAS STILL A LONG WAY OFF, HIS FATHER SAW HIM AND WAS FILLED WITH COMPASSION FOR HIM; HE RAN TO HIS SON, THREW HIS ARMS AROUND HIM AND KISSED HIM. THE SON SAID TO HIM, "FATHER, I HAVE SINNED AGAINST HEAVEN AND AGAINST YOU. I AM NO LONGER WORTHY TO BE CALLED YOUR SON."

LUKE 15:20–21

Now we come to the ultimate test of friendship with our adult children. Can we continue to nurture a healthy friendship with our children when we don't agree with their choices? Remember that this book focuses on developing successful relationships with our children, not having successful children. Visible success is separate from true spiritual success—having an intimate relationship with Jesus Christ—which may develop by taking different paths. We wholeheartedly embrace the parable of the lost son in Scripture (Luke 15:11–32), knowing that God holds out open arms to us, yet we don't want to accept that sometimes we must live out this reality with our own children. We have to be the parent with open arms. We also empathize with the good son who has remained faithful to his father. No one throws a party for him.

When high school student Erica learned that she was pregnant, the first person she told was her mom. Erica wanted to keep her baby, and her parents decided to help Erica raise him. Lisa was a college student when she became pregnant. She immediately sought out the guidance of her parents. Lisa's mom became her birth coach and helped Lisa navigate the difficult decision to give up her baby for adoption. When Melissa learned of her pregnancy, she didn't want anyone, especially her parents, to know. She went to a clinic to have an abortion.

This book is not about raising children who do not make mistakes. That is an unreachable goal. We have a universal need for a savior because we are all imperfect, broken human beings. Some of our struggles are simply more visible than others. We know from personal experience that these struggles often bring us closer to God. We learn to depend on Him completely.

If it were up to us and we had to choose between our children living problem-free, struggle-free lives or experiencing an intimate relationship with Jesus Christ, which would we choose? What sane parents would not want both for their children? It frees us to realize that this is not our choice to make. We trust that God holds our children in His hands, just as He holds us.

When we disagree with our children's choices, we need to continue to extend friendship by keeping communication lines open, practicing patience, offering unconditional love and forgiveness, and mirroring the compassion of Jesus Christ by having heart vision.

KEEPING COMMUNICATION LINES OPEN

BEING A POSTPARENT REQUIRES A DIFFERENT SET OF SKILLS, NEW RULES FOR NEW ROLES.

> EVEN IF YOUR KIDS ARE OUT OF YOUR HOUSE,
> THEY'RE STILL IN YOUR HEART, AND THEY
> ALWAYS WILL BE.
>
> JANE ADAMS

In healthy friendships, we feel safe to openly share our failures and struggles. Since this book focuses on nurturing friendships with our adult children, we must ask ourselves, "Do my children openly and honestly share their struggles with me?"

No matter how hard we tried to be good parents, our adult children sometimes make choices that we do not agree with or cannot support biblically. As dedicated parents, we hoped to protect our children from unnecessary pain and regret by teaching them to follow biblical guidelines. We don't understand why our scriptural guidance was ignored. Yet even in difficult situations we can remain friends and keep the lines of communication open. In doing so, we provide our children with a positive, Christlike influence. These are the same actions we would take if any other friend was struggling or in crisis. We cannot instantly solve our friends' problems but we can be there for them in the midst of the problems.

Parents who cut off relationships with struggling adult children intending to send the message, "Shape up now," usually cut off the ability to influence them. The result is too often a permanently terminated relationship. When Marie and Tom learned that their daughter, Kara, had moved in with her non-Christian boyfriend, they made it clear that they would not condone them as a couple. They refused to spend time with Kara's boyfriend. Soon Marie and Tom were not spending time with their daughter either. Kara has now been estranged from her parents for several years and she still lives with her boyfriend.

When Lydia and Michael faced the same situation with their daughter, Tanya, they were as heartbroken as Marie and Tom. Yet Lydia and Michael painfully decided to embrace their daughter's boyfriend. They lived out their faith in front of the couple and over-whelmed Tanya's boyfriend with love. The couples attended church together. When Tanya's relationship with her boyfriend ended, Tanya's faith had grown as well as her friendship with her parents.

Mary Ann's story mirrors the experience of many parents today. She and her husband seemed to have the ideal daughter. Rachel had a strong faith, was close to her family, excelled in school, and was accepted to a respected university. Mary Ann shared with me:

> After Rachel left to attend college, we learned that she was meeting young men online. She desperately wanted to have a romantic relationship. We understood that desire but were puzzled why she wasn't trying to meet male students on campus. Rachel then became involved online with a young man who lived in another part of our state. Soon they were traveling to visit one another.
>
> Jason was everything that Rachel wasn't. He was a nonbeliever, did not attend college, and had a minimum wage job. We were baffled and thought their relationship would run its course after Rachel explored having her first boyfriend. My husband and I kept lovingly sharing our concerns with Rachel. We diligently prayed for her. I questioned where our parenting had gone wrong. Yet Jason and Rachel only became more serious.
>
> Then my husband and I realized that we had to make an important decision. We could alienate our daughter and lose our relationship or we could encourage her to be open with us, accepting her choice though we didn't agree with it. We completely surrendered her to God.

We decided to love Jason as Christ loves him. When Rachel called to tell me about Jason's proposal, I wanted to be thrilled for her but I wasn't. Planning the wedding was not a joyous experience. My heart was heavy. We knew that God was calling us to disciple Jason. He would be the father of our grandchildren.

After their marriage, Rachel and Jason attended church with us. Two years later, Jason was baptized and he asked us to participate in his baptism as his spiritual parents. Today we meet weekly for a Bible study in our home. Other nights they join us to play games. We have become close friends.

Kaitlyn's parents were concerned when Kaitlyn dated and married Joshua. Joshua was a solid believer but he was also a recovering alcoholic and took medication for bipolar disorder. He had trouble holding a steady job. When Joshua was sober, properly medicated, and employed, he was a wonderful man and husband. He was the perfect example of a man rescued by Jesus Christ. When Joshua lost his job due to the recession and began to struggle, he turned his anger and frustration on Kaitlyn. Though Joshua and Kaitlyn shared their common faith, soon their marriage was unraveling. Kaitlyn's parents feared for their daughter's safety and were only less devastated than Joshua's parents.

While Mary Ann's story has a happy ending, many others do not. Some result in abuse, divorce, poverty, addiction, serious illness, and lasting heartache. What these parents have in common is they decide to continue working on a friendship with their children and their partners. That commitment is not dependent on circumstances. They accept their children's choices even though they disagree with them.

Lucy remembers that her parents told her thirty years ago not to marry her boyfriend. When she did marry him, her parents said, "You've made a bad choice but now it's done. Don't ever come crying to us when you have problems." Lucy and her children lived with an abusive husband and father for years because she felt she had no options and could not confide in her parents.

PRACTICING PATIENCE

> **TRUE COURAGE IS CHARACTERIZED BY PATIENCE —PATIENCE WITH GOD, WHOSE WORK IS OFTEN IMPERCEPTIBLE AND SLOW.**
>
> GORDON SMITH

Our adult children sometimes make choices that are not unbiblical but simply unwise in our opinion. They may experience failure, which is often God's best teaching tool. Because we are friends, we do not rescue our children or fix their problems, but we can still lovingly encourage them. As mature adults, we have learned that failure to reach one's original goal can result in opened doors to better opportunities. Life's detours often prove superior to our original plans, and in hindsight, we see God's fingerprints all over our lives. Adult children need to experience this revelation for themselves.

Parents can have successful friendships with their children, even when baffled by their children's life choices, if they remain patient. The key is to understand that God's timetable is usually different from our own. In our culture of immediate gratification, we desire overnight change, but God is never in a hurry. Since God is not in a hurry, we should trust that He sees the big picture. Peter reminds us that a day is like a thousand years to the Lord (2 Peter 3:8). Getting instant results is not God's method. He longs for enduring results and transformed lives.

Ron tried to do everything right as a parent. He made the conscious choice to build a relationship with his children that he did not experience with his own father. Instead of being critical, he was affirming and supportive. Instead of being dictatorial, Ron led by example and earned the right to influence them. He was a positive role model. Instead of being unplugged, Ron was engaged and involved in all his children's activities at school and church. He cheered them on as they pursued their passions. Ron and his wife invested well in their children and trusted that their purposeful parenting would make a difference in their lives.

When their firstborn son, Michael, attended a respected Christian university to major in computer science, Ron and his wife had high hopes for his future. They knew how capable and intelligent their son was. To their dismay, after Michael graduated from college, he did not pursue his career choice. He started working at night in a minimum wage job. Ron hoped that this was simply a phase, but as time passed and Michael never looked for a job in his field, Ron realized that Michael had chosen to simply exist, take no risks, and invest the least amount of effort in his life. Michael played computer games, lived a sedentary lifestyle, and gained weight.

Ron and his wife were baffled, disappointed, and heartbroken for their son. They knew Michael's decision to waste his potential would severely limit his future life choices. In reaction to his own father's constant criticism, Ron had embraced the popular advice, "Don't major on the minors. Pick your battles carefully." In hindsight, Ron wondered if he picked his battles so carefully that he didn't even engage in the war.

At age twenty-nine, Michael asked his parents for permission to move home. Ron and his wife wrestled with the decision and allowed Michael to move home under certain conditions. They placed a time limit on his stay. Within a few months, Michael would need to find a job and a new place to live, and develop a solid plan to recover from financial debt. Ron labeled these few months "Launch #2."

Michael made choices that were unwise in Ron's opinion, but Ron was patient and kept the lines of communication open with Michael. After Michael moved out and met all their conditions, he continued to visit his parents weekly to spend family time together and study the Bible. Patience helped Ron remain friends with his son, even though he didn't always agree with his choices.

> BUT DO NOT FORGET THIS ONE THING, DEAR FRIENDS: WITH THE LORD A DAY IS LIKE A THOUSAND YEARS, AND A THOUSAND YEARS ARE LIKE A DAY. THE LORD IS NOT SLOW IN KEEPING HIS PROMISE, AS SOME UNDERSTAND SLOWNESS. HE IS PATIENT WITH YOU, NOT WANTING ANYONE TO PERISH, BUT EVERYONE TO COME TO REPENTANCE.
>
> 2 PETER 3:8–9

OFFERING UNCONDITIONAL LOVE AND FORGIVENESS

> OUR ABILITY TO FORGIVE IS IN DIRECT PROPORTION TO OUR GENUINE IDENTITY WITH CHRIST. OUR RELUCTANCE TO FORGIVE REFLECTS THE DISTANCE IN OUR RELATIONSHIP WITH CHRIST.
>
> CHUCK LYNCH

Friendship with our adult children can transcend the deepest heartache. We can be friends with our children without condoning or enabling their behavior. We can lovingly encourage them as they suffer the consequences of their actions. Many remarkable parents understand that nurturing a friendship with one's children does not translate into approval of their choices. It does not mean rescuing them from painful consequences. What it does entail is extending to adult children the unconditional love and forgiveness that parents receive from God.

On her Saturday outings, Lisa fights the sadness as she watches other mothers and daughters shopping and laughing together. She and her husband, Chris, tried to have a child for several years. After medical intervention failed, they decided to adopt. After a long process, they finally adopted an infant girl, given up by her mother who suffered with drug addiction. Lisa and Chris were thrilled to finally be parents, and lavished love and attention on their daughter, Mallory. Growing up in a loving, Christian home, Mallory could not have had more dedicated parents. Yet when Mallory became a teenager, the nightmare began, almost as if a switch had been flipped. She began to experiment with drugs, alcohol, and sex, threaten suicide, run away in the middle of the night, and turn her anger on her parents. Lisa and Chris enlisted every resource to help Mallory. They learned that several members of her biological family suffered with addiction and mental illness.

Lisa and Chris believed they had been chosen by God to love their daughter and help Mallory fight her DNA. They placed Mallory in special schools and hospitals, with treatment from the best doctors and therapists. When she continued to run away and put herself in dangerous situations, Lisa and Chris made the difficult decision to place Mallory in an out-of-state facility, where her safety was assured. They stayed in contact weekly and made regular trips to visit Mallory. Their constant message was, "Just as God loves you, we will never stop loving you and promise to keep you safe." When Mallory returned home from her program, Lisa and Chris were hopeful about her future, yet Mallory could not stay clean. A few months later, Mallory became a legal adult. Lisa and Chris no longer had the legal right to make decisions for Mallory. They continued to unconditionally love her but refused to rescue her or fund her decline and allowed her to face the painful consequences of her adult actions.

Leslie made regular visits to see her son, Ryan, when he was in prison. Ryan has a solid faith in Jesus Christ, knowing what he has been rescued from. He suffers from chemical imbalances, addiction, and the consequences of poor choices. Leslie proves that parents can be good friends with their adult children while not condoning their behavior. Leslie sent books to Ryan to encourage his faith during his incarceration. Ryan witnessed to other inmates and asked for his parents' guidance in following his Lord. No matter the pain they have endured on earth, Leslie and her husband, Shawn, know that they will spend eternity with their son. Shawn had often taken his sons on summer camping trips to spend uninterrupted father/son time together. After Ryan was released from prison, he and his dad embarked on another camping trip to help ground him for the challenges ahead.

Parents who are able to unconditionally love and befriend their prodigal children are often mature believers, grounded in the truth of Scripture. They understand that parents are not held responsible for the brokenness of their children, nor are children held responsible for the brokenness of their parents (Deuteronomy 24:16; Ezekiel 18:5–20; John 9:1–4). The theme of Ezekiel chapter 18 is personal responsibility before God: "A son is not to suffer for the sins of his father, nor a father for the sins of his son" (v. 20 JB).

Parents of prodigal children also understand that they extend the forgiveness that they receive from God. They know that forgiveness is not optional. God commands us to forgive one another (Matthew 6:14–15; Mark 11:25). They know that forgiveness is a daily decision, a process requiring practice. Philip Yancey writes, "Forgiveness must be taught and practiced, as one would practice any difficult craft."[1] They don't confuse forgiveness with tolerating abuse or enabling destructive behavior.

Forgiveness is not forgetting. Forgivers choose to not remember, the way that God forgives us: "I will forgive their wickedness, and will remember their sins no more" (Jeremiah 31:34). "Forgetting" is a passive response. "Not remembering" is an active choice. It is preventive forgiveness. Parents who have remained friends with their adult children told me how they handled painful slights to deep rejection:

- I chose not to be offended.
- I chose not to be hurt.
- I chose not to notice.
- I chose not to remember.

Most parents know the pain of a slight, such as being forgotten on a holiday or birthday or not being thanked for a gift or acknowledged for a sacrifice made. Other parents live with the deep pain of rejection and being estranged. Parents must realize that God's command to forgive others includes forgiving our adult children. They are not exempt.[2]

> BEAR WITH EACH OTHER AND FORGIVE WHATEVER GRIEVANCES YOU MAY HAVE AGAINST ONE ANOTHER. FORGIVE AS THE LORD FORGAVE YOU. AND OVER ALL THESE VIRTUES PUT ON LOVE, WHICH BINDS THEM ALL TOGETHER IN PERFECT UNITY.
>
> COLOSSIANS 3:13–14

HEART VISION—MIRRORING THE COMPASSION OF CHRIST

> FORGIVENESS OPENS THE DOOR AND COMPASSION WALKS THROUGH IT.
>
> CHUCK LYNCH

Imagine that your adult son is having an affair with a married woman. He then arranges the murder of her husband. You poured your life into raising your son and realize that he is an adulterer, schemer, murderer, liar, criminal, and appears beyond redemption. We understand that God experienced this disappointment with David. We read in 2 Samuel 13 that David's son, Amnon, raped his virgin sister, Tamar, and David did nothing to discipline Amnon. We watch David continually fail and collapse in weakness, and we view God's endless response of forgiveness. What I personally bristle at is God's affirmation that David has been faithful to the Lord and "done what was right in the eyes of the Lord and had not disobeyed any of his commandments all his life, except in the matter of Uriah the Hittite" (1 Kings 15:5 NEB). Did that deceit and murder matter so little? I look at David's track record and think, "He was often not an obedient, faithful servant."

In spite of all his failures, David loved and tried to follow God. Through David's constant struggles, God loved him. God sees the heart. We human parents too often see only the actions of our children. We need to see our children through God's eyes. We need heart vision.

One veteran mother explains:

> I have known many loving Christian parents who tried every approach to help their struggling adult children. A few of them live with the deep grief of losing their children. One young man overdosed. Another committed suicide. Sometimes families are estranged and parents don't know if their children are dead or alive.
>
> When my own adult children left home and began to struggle, I realized that our relationship had to take precedence over parental instruction or moral teaching. The most important gifts we

can give our prodigal children are unconditional love, mercy, grace, and compassion so that they can find their way home when they have nowhere else to turn. This is the most powerful biblical portrait we have of our Father's unending love for us.

When we disagree with our children's choices is when we most need to practice heart vision and extend friendship by keeping communication lines open, being patient, offering unconditional love and forgiveness, and mirroring the compassion of Jesus Christ. When our children struggle is when they most need an anchor.

> PARENTHOOD IS ONE LONG EXERCISE IN RELINQUISHING CONTROL, OR THE ILLUSION IF WE EVER HAD IT. POST-PARENTHOOD, BY CONTRAST, IS ABOUT ACCEPTANCE. ONE OF THE HARDEST THINGS FOR ANY PARENT TO ACCEPT IS THAT NO MATTER HOW MUCH VIGILANCE WE EXERCISE, WE CANNOT ALWAYS CONTROL WHAT HAPPENS TO OUR CHILDREN. FOR EVEN THOUGH WE PUT PLUGS IN ALL THE SOCKETS, THEY GOT SHOCKED. AND EVEN THOUGH WE PUT GATES ON TOP OF THE STAIRS, THEY FELL. AND EVEN THOUGH WE TAUGHT THEM TO SAY NO TO THE THINGS THAT WERE BAD FOR THEM, SOMETIMES THEY SAY YES.
>
> JANE ADAMS

A mother shares:

After watching my dad and teenage brother experience deep division in their relationship over my brother's long hair and other insignificant issues, I firmly believed that externals should not be the focus when raising my own children. Character was much more important than what my teens wore or what color they dyed their hair. It was challenging to bite my tongue when my daughter dyed her beautiful blonde hair a variety of colors—black, purple, and orange. I also bit my tongue when my sons pierced their nipples to wear rings. It was difficult to hear church friends voice their opinions about my children's appearance.

Our family focused on intentionally spending time together and respecting one another. My husband and I often read Scripture and great works of literature out loud to our children. My husband took our sons on an annual backpacking trip to discuss life issues. We also went on camping trips as a family. We always encouraged our children to be honest with us and even listened to input about our parenting. We welcomed their questions and insights. Sometimes we had family meetings to discuss conflicts and problems. Everyone could share their views without interruption. We each listened to each other and then discussed solutions.

My husband and I realized when we had young children that we had very different skills in parenting. I was the planner who could help them finish tasks. My husband was the listener who could listen to them for hours. Our children learned which parent they should seek out depending on the challenges they faced.

Regardless of our adult children's choices, including some we have been saddened by, we have chosen to unconditionally love them, giving them grace, not condemnation. One of our children has walked far away from God, yet I know that God will not completely let go of him. Our children know where we stand on biblical beliefs; we don't have to tell them. We know that their journey is between them and God, and we can trust Him to guide them. Trusting God is what frees us to love and support them as our beloved children.

A mother shares:

We wanted our children to know that they were always loved no matter what they did. I think that each of us craves that unconditional love, the love that only God can truly give us. Yet we parents can model that so our children will have a taste of the Father's love for them. We certainly disciplined and guided our children as they grew up. When they became adults, we did not bail them out financially, no matter how hard it was to watch them struggle, so that they learned to be financially independent. After our children were grown, we kept our mouths shut, loving them even when we didn't agree with their choices. We extended love to our son's spouse, even when she hurt our son. We were heartbroken when our daughter moved in with her boyfriend, but we extended love to him and kept communication open with our daughter. Our children already knew where we stood on following and obeying God.

We focused on having a friendship with our children. Because what is a friend? It is someone who knows us and loves us anyway.

A mother shares:

My husband and I did our best to follow God in raising our three children. We had daily devotions with them, attended church together, and sent them to private, conservative Christian schools. We encouraged their faith. We laid the foundation for friendship in many ways. My husband coached our son's baseball team. We went on family vacations and valued family time. We ate dinner together as a family. As our children became adults, we stayed in regular contact, invited them to visit, and also visited them. Our faith in Jesus

Christ has been central to developing friendship with our children. We believe that family is a gift from God and is worth fighting for as we nurture healthy relationships.

We are good friends with our eldest son, Brett, and his wife. They seek out ways to spend time with us and even invited us to go on two cruises with them. That's proof of friendship to us. Brett was easy to raise and now I realize that we can't take all the credit for that. He is a big, tall, lovable teddy bear with whom we have always had a good relationship. He excelled in school, graduated from college in four years, graduated from law school and passed the bar on his first try, and is financially, personally, and professionally successful.

Today we are good friends with our adult daughter, Megan, but we suffered through several years of pain and hardship to remain in relationship with her. We believed in loving her unconditionally yet sometimes had to practice tough love in her best interest. It was a constant balancing act. When Megan chose to live with her boyfriend who was involved with drugs, we told her that we didn't approve but nothing could stop us from loving her or spending time with her. We felt helpless as we watched her become embroiled in the drugs lifestyle. After she became pregnant, she and her boyfriend married but the nightmare continued. We became devoted grandparents to a precious little girl. We wanted to remain a lifeline for our daughter and her family.

Soon Megan learned that her husband was having an affair with her friend. In the midst of living with his lies, drug use, and cheating, Megan learned that she was pregnant with their second child. She finally decided to leave her husband, a decision we completely supported. Megan and her two children came to live with us. We became good friends with our daughter, developed a close bond with our grandchildren, and enjoyed peaceful years together. Today Megan is married to a wonderful man who treats her well and loves her children as his own. I miraculously met this man while traveling and introduced them. I constantly thank God for the happy ending to her story.

We are not good friends with our youngest adult son . . . yet. He still lives in our home. He started dabbling with drugs in high school and we fear that he continues his drug use. He is unsure about his future plans. We are not fighting but we are not communicating either. I pray to God for wisdom and the right words to help him. I realize now that three children can be raised in the same household with similar faith and values, yet their journeys can take separate paths and our friendships with them can be equally different. Treating them with the same unconditional love is the common thread to preserving a good relationship for the future. God knows that our children are in process.

The love of our neighbor in all its fullness simply means being able to say to him: "What are you going through?"

Simone Weil

In my mother's generation, a mother's role was solely to guide and protect, not to share her personal experiences or problems the way a dear friend would. It was taboo for a mother to tell her daughter that she felt depressed or afraid . . . But once a woman reaches adulthood, an added benefit of having a mother is the potential for friendship. The opportunity to exchange thoughts and intimate feelings helps both women explore solutions to problems and ask and answer difficult or meaningful questions about life.

Mary Marcdante

The more a daughter knows the details of her mother's life—without flinching or whining—the stronger the daughter.

Anita Diamant

EIGHT

BEING A FRIEND AND ENCOURAGER

NEVER UNDERESTIMATE THE POWER
OF ONE PERSON TO REDIRECT A CHILD
TOWARD A MORE PRODUCTIVE, SUCCESSFUL,
SATISFYING LIFE. AS PARENTS, WE MUST
FIND WAYS IN WHICH TO HELP CHILDREN
FEEL SPECIAL AND APPRECIATED WITHOUT
INDULGING THEM.
ROBERT BROOKS AND SAM GOLDSTEIN

Once we have laid the foundation for adult friendship, started treating our children as adult friends, and let go completely, we have the privilege of coming alongside them to encourage them. We can compassionately minister to them, not worrying that we will cripple them with kindness.

In Philemon 1:7, Paul describes Philemon as one whose "love has given me great joy and encouragement, because you, brother, have refreshed the hearts of the saints." To en*courage* is to bestow courage. To re*fresh* is to make fresh and ready for action. When we provide refreshment to discouraged people, we revive and replenish them. Philemon did both for Paul and other believers.

My favorite definition of an encourager is Paul's description of Onesiphorus:

> May the Lord show mercy to the household of
> Onesiphorus, because he often refreshed me and

was not ashamed of my chains. On the contrary, when he was in Rome, he searched hard for me until he found me. May the Lord grant that he will find mercy from the Lord on that day! You know very well in how many ways he helped me in Ephesus. (2 Timothy 1:16–18)

Onesiphorus encouraged his friend by:

1.   Often refreshing Paul.
2.   Not being ashamed or embarrassed of Paul while he was imprisoned.
3.   Searching for Paul, never giving up until he found him.
4.   Helping Paul in many tangible ways.

Onesiphorus made every effort to encourage, help, and remain in relationship with Paul, no matter Paul's circumstances. Contrast Onesiphorus with Alexander the metal worker who deeply hurt Paul, and everyone who deserted Paul when he needed their support (2 Timothy 4:14–16).

Like Philemon and Onesiphorus, we too are called to come alongside others, offering comfort, encouragement, and refreshment. When life is painful or challenging, the kind words or thoughtful acts of a compassionate friend can make all the difference. Proverbs teaches that "a kindly glance gives joy to the heart, good news lends strength to the bones" (15:30 JB). We want to minister to our adult children as we would minister to any friend, encouraging them along the journey.

OFFERING COMFORT, NOT HEARTACHE

A MERRY HEART MAKES A CHEERFUL FACE; HEARTACHE CRUSHES THE SPIRIT.

PROVERBS 15:13 NEB

We do not want to be a source of heartache or discouragement for our children. Paul warns, "Fathers, do not embitter your children, or they will become discouraged" (Colossians 3:21). Instead, we want to build them up rather than pull them down (2 Corinthians 10:8). We want to lighten their load. Parents can reflect one aspect of the Holy Spirit's work. An important term used to describe the Holy Spirit in the New Testament is *Paraclete* (John 14:16; 16:7), which comes from the Greek word *paráklētos* meaning "one who comes alongside us." Here is the best summation from Paul of biblical goals for parents:

> You are witnesses, and so is God, of how holy,
> righteous and blameless we were among you who
> believed. For you know that we dealt with each
> of you as a father deals with his own children,
> encouraging, comforting and urging you to live
> lives worthy of God, who call you into his king-
> dom and glory. (1 Thessalonians 2:10–12)

Our goals are to encourage and comfort, thus urging our adult children to live lives worthy of God.

Observe that urging them to live godly lives is intertwined with offering them encouragement and comfort. Without palpable love, our efforts are ineffective. In 1 Thessalonians 2:6–7, Paul describes his ministry as gentle: "As apostles of Christ we could have been a burden to you, but we were gentle among you, like a mother caring for her little children." In this letter to the church of the Thessalonians, Paul pours out his love as a parent would. One mother says, "My adult children's lives are already hard and stressful enough. I want to ease their load, not add to it." This mother enjoys hosting her daughter and son-in-law for dinner one night a week, after their long work days. Another mother sets aside every Saturday morning to take her young grandchildren to the park so that her son and daughter-in-law can go out for breakfast to recover from their busy week and discuss plans for the next week.

HEALTHY GIFT GIVING

> "IF YOU THEN, THOUGH YOU ARE EVIL, KNOW HOW TO GIVE GOOD GIFTS TO YOUR CHILDREN, HOW MUCH MORE WILL YOUR FATHER IN HEAVEN GIVE THE HOLY SPIRIT TO THOSE WHO ASK HIM!"
>
> LUKE 11:13

Parents are sometimes unsure how to navigate the difference between giving good gifts to their children and rescuing them. A gift is given freely, not demanded by the receiver. Ideally the gift is received with a grateful heart. Healthy gift giving is radically different from bailing people out. Allowing adults to experience consequences needed for their own growth is a different type of gift. We are talking about freely offering presents as expressions of goodwill, friendship, and affection, with no strings attached. These gifts are tangible ways to encourage others.

Parents have described their pleasure in giving gifts to their adult children by saying, "I love to make them smile," "I love to surprise them," and "I love to lift their spirits on a hard day." Samantha says that the key to giving good gifts is carefully observing and listening to children as they express their heart's desires. Many parents enjoy sending regular care packages to their adult children who live far from home. One mother scoped out the various businesses in her son's town. Every month she sent him gift certificates to a store, coffee shop, restaurant, or movie theater.

Finding opportunities to encourage our adult children builds on the foundation we set during their childhood (see chapter 3). Whether we attended the opening day of baseball season each year or celebrated our children's half-birthdays, the special events, family traditions, private jokes, weekly rituals, or annual trips we once shared are ways to continue connecting with our children when they no longer live at home. Perhaps we can still purchase two opening day tickets, treat our children to a celebratory dinner, or plan the annual summer camping trip. We may have to find new, creative ways to celebrate them on special days if they live far away, like sending packages or traveling to see them. What they will appreciate is that we make the effort to remember them. Pampering and encouraging them, with the tender loving care we would extend to any close friend, is appropriate only because our children are independent, self-sufficient adults.

Parents who give gifts to their children model a generous spirit. We find it rewarding to watch our children follow our example and give gifts to encourage the people in their lives. Even more rewarding is when they surprise us with a gift or pay for a restaurant bill. We realize that we are enjoying a mutual friendship. Proverbs 11:25 states, "The generous soul will prosper, he who waters, will be watered" (JB).

Healthy gift giving does not expect a return on one's investment. Followers of Jesus Christ are called to be generous givers, with no hidden expectations. When children are young, most parents enjoy rewarding them with special treats and gifts. This is how we reinforce good behavior. In contrast, gifts of encouragement for adult children are not bribes or rewards. Leslie sends Christian books and Bibles to her son in prison to encourage his faith. When adults most struggle is when they most need encouragement.

Tamara entered a deep depression when she was laid off from her job and her husband left her without warning. Tamara did not ask her parents for help. She did not want to move home and become a burden to them. Knowing that Tamara was devastated and unable to reach out for help, her parents looked for ways to encourage her, through regularly calling her, offering invitations for meals, and leaving her gifts of money and groceries at her apartment. Their gifts and attention communicated that they love their daughter and are always there for her. She is not alone.

A MAN'S SPIRIT MAY SUSTAIN HIM IN SICKNESS, BUT IF THE SPIRIT IS WOUNDED, WHO CAN MEND IT? KNOWLEDGE COMES TO THE DISCERNING MIND; THE WISE EAR LISTENS TO GET KNOWLEDGE. A GIFT OPENS THE DOOR TO THE GIVER AND GAINS ACCESS TO THE GREAT.

PROVERBS 18:14–16 NEB

THE GIFT OF SPIRITUAL HUGS

WHENEVER THE INSISTENCE IS ON THE POINT THAT GOD ANSWERS PRAYER, WE ARE OFF THE TRACK. THE MEANING OF PRAYER IS THAT WE GET HOLD OF GOD, NOT OF THE ANSWER.

OSWALD CHAMBERS

When our adult children live far away or we cannot speak with them about uncomfortable topics, we can always pray for them, wrapping them in spiritual hugs. We can pray for God to protect them (spiritually, physically, mentally, and emotionally) and guide them in all areas of life. Stormie Omartian writes,

> We parents of adult children may have many concerns, but not necessarily the opening to do anything about them, or even the opportunity to voice all our thoughts, suggestions, and opinions. At least not to our adult children. But we do have a grand opening to be able to express those concerns to God and invite Him to do something about them. And the greatest thing about that is, when we take our concerns to the Lord—trusting that God hears our prayers and answers them on

> behalf of our adult children—it means our prayers
> have power to affect change in their lives. And
> that gives us a peace we can find no other way.[1]

We must remember to pray for our children in accordance with God's will, not for what we perceive is best for them (i.e., in accordance with our will). We also realize that the first people that prayer changes is ourselves. We engage in an intimate two-way conversation with our Lord. As a result, when we are right with God, listen to His voice, and mirror Jesus Christ, all our relationships benefit as well.

You may be familiar with phrases such as, "I pray for God to intervene in my child's life," or "I released him into God's hands." That affords parents too much power, as if God remains absent from our children's lives without our reminding Him. We can trust that God always has His hand firmly on the shoulders of our children. He has a relationship with them that is completely separate from our relationship with Him.

As much as we love our children, God loves them infinitely more. He is their ultimate parent and rescuer. Jesus Christ is their sufficient intercessor. God sees our children when we can't. He protects them when we can't. He sees the big picture of their lives when we can't see tomorrow. God knows better than we do when our children are following Him closely or walking far away from Him.

We pray to wrap our children in spiritual hugs and envelop them with the blanket of God's presence, guidance, protection, and comfort, which is powerful encouragement, especially when they are experiencing tough times. A parent who prays throughout the day (and often during late-night hours) for his or her adult children offers them a priceless gift.

THE GIFT OF ENCOURAGING WORDS

> TAKING THE TIME TO GATHER LITTLE PIECES OF
> LOVE, GRACE, STRENGTH, AND HOPE IS WORTH
> IT WHEN YOU SHOWER YOUR FRIENDSHIPS
> WITH THEM. ENCOURAGEMENT IS TO FRIEND-
> SHIP WHAT CONFETTI IS TO A PARTY. IT'S LIGHT,
> REFRESHING, AND FUN, AND YOU ALWAYS END
> UP FINDING LITTLE PIECES OF IT STUCK ON YOU
> LATER.
>
> NICOLE JOHNSON

Encouraging words are also valuable gifts. We can reread written words for a lifetime to comfort us. Sometimes we vividly remember and carry in our hearts powerful spoken words of kindness and affirmation. On rare occasions, one significant statement of encouragement can change the course of a young person's life. One woman explains:

> During my senior year in high school, I sat crying through my final exam in history class. Instead of being upset with me, my teacher called me outside the classroom to ask what was wrong. I told him that my boyfriend had been unfaithful. Coming from a home without supportive parents, I had wrapped up my life in my boyfriend and now felt like I'd been thrown away. My teacher simply asked, "What do *you* want in life?" No one had ever asked me that before. He suggested that I use this breakup as an opportunity to follow my dreams and start over. He encouraged me to attend college. Four days later, I moved

across the state, enrolled in college courses, and started a new life. My life was changed because one person cared.[2]

In chapter 4, we realized that what we say is as important as what we don't say. Holding our tongues is critical to nurturing friendship with our adult children. Yet the reverse is also true and may be more powerful. To withhold kind, encouraging words can be as damaging as making cruel, hurtful statements. Our goal is to share generous doses of "honey words" and eliminate "weapon words." Proverbs 16:24 reads, "Kind words are like dripping honey, sweetness on the tongue and health for the body" (NEB). Proverbs 12:18 reads, "There are some whose thoughtless words pierce like a sword, but the tongue of the wise brings healing" (JB).

Some adults have shared with me that they knew their parents deeply loved them, generously provided and cared for them, and were always there for them, but they rarely spoke kind, encouraging words to them. Their weapon words far outweighed their honey words. One adult described this experience as "verbal poverty," although she grew up in an affluent lifestyle.

Glenn O'Connor works as an airport chaplain, available to comfort stressed travelers. Sometimes he helps people in the midst of crisis, such as illness or the loss of a loved one. Other times, he is a sounding board for frustrated travelers experiencing delayed or cancelled flights. He speaks honey words as a ministry and vocation. O'Connor calls his work the "ministry of presence." He is simply there to provide a listening ear and tangible assistance. Whatever the traveler is going through, he or she is no longer feels alone.

Navigating a busy airport seems an appropriate analogy, as our adult children come and go on numerous life journeys. Like Chaplain O'Connor, may we too practice the ministry of presence, comfort, and encouragement.

HE DIED FOR US SO THAT, WHETHER WE ARE AWAKE OR ASLEEP, WE MAY LIVE TOGETHER WITH HIM. THEREFORE ENCOURAGE ONE ANOTHER AND BUILD EACH OTHER UP, JUST AS IN FACT YOU ARE DOING.

1 THESSALONIANS 5:10–11

A mother shares:

During my children's Toastmasters Club, I noticed a mother taking notes on her clipboard while her children were presenting. At the top of her paper was written, "What was wrong." Abraham Lincoln said, "If you look for the worst in people and expect to find it, you surely will." I believe that the key to becoming friends with my adult children is focusing on their strengths and seeing the best in them. I boldly brag about them.

When my children were young, our family often played the Greatness Game. We took turns focusing on one another, saying out loud the greatness we saw in each other. My adult children still need to hear about their positive qualities and be praised for their triumphs. Pointing out negative qualities only sabotages relationships.

Since I grew up in an abusive, dysfunctional home, I experienced the pain of living with parents who only see the worst in their child. I grew up knowing that I wasn't worth their effort. I cannot remember my mom or dad saying a kind, affirming word to me or about me to other people. I was determined that each of my children would feel like a priceless treasure, never a worthless inconvenience. My children know that they are a priority in my life, worth all my effort. I offer my adult children unconditional love with no strings attached or expectations. Their voices are heard and their opinions count. When I don't agree with their choices, I realize that everyone needs grace and a safe place with no judgment or criticism. One of my daughters taught me, "Mom, just listen. Don't try to fix anything."

My adult children live all over the United States. I work at maintaining frequent, pleasant contact with each of them through texting, calling, sending care packages, and planning annual family trips. I am paid the highest compliment when my children include me in their fun plans. When I moved, I gave each of my children a key to my new house. My home will always be a safe place for them.

Her adult daughter shares:

I am close friends with my mom. We talk often, about anything and everything. We have a mutually supportive relationship, letting each other vent when needed or cheering each other on in a new adventure. I can't go for more than a few days without talking to her. Our contact is not a "have to" but a "want to."

My mom lets me make my own decisions. She will offer advice but doesn't force it on me. We give each other permission to change and grow. She respects me as an adult and lets me live my life without judgment. Even when we don't agree, we stay in contact and still talk. If I ever need anything, she is there for me, no questions asked. I trust my mom 100 percent.

A mother shares:

In our fast-paced, high-tech society, too few people are making deep connections. I did not have a soul connection with my stay-at-home mom even in the pre-digital age, which is why I was determined to have that connection with my daughters. I didn't want them to feel isolated as I did. Neither my husband's parents nor my parents chose to be involved grandparents in our children's lives. Someday my husband and I would like to purchase homes near each of our daughters so that we can regularly visit them and our grandchildren. We will purposefully nurture those family relationships.

I had the privilege of not missing one moment in my daughters' lives, from their first steps to their first day of school to their college graduation, and every event in between. We have an intimate connection. Today my adult daughters cheer me on in my late-life career, instruct me how to use technology, give me quirky gifts that only we understand, and share lots of hugs, love, and laughter with me. I feel that I have won the grand prize to be on the receiving end of their adult love. You get back what you give out. It's that simple.

An adult daughter shares:

I am good friends with my mom. She is also my mentor and inspiration. She has a strong faith and I admire her. I grew up involved in various volunteer projects, working alongside my mom. She started a neighborhood watch, raised funds to restore a community theater, and organized many church events. Today she grows food in a community garden for a food pantry and raises funds for a Christian camp. She's always on the go yet she is never too busy to sit on the back porch and talk with me.

Don't worry that children never listen to you. Worry that they are always watching you.

Robert Fulghum

Mentoring, at least when practiced by Christians, certainly ought to center everything on Christ. But mentoring is less about instruction than it is about initiation—about bringing young men into maturity. Whereas the word for disciple means "learner," the word protégé comes from a Latin word meaning "to protect." The mentor aims to protect his young charge as he crosses the frontier into manhood. For my own part, I do not make a hard and fast distinction between discipleship and mentoring. There is a great deal of overlap. But I like the concept of mentoring because it focuses on relationships.

Howard Hendricks and William Hendricks

Even though you have ten thousand guardians in Christ, you do not have many fathers, for in Christ Jesus I became your father through the gospel. Therefore I urge you to imitate me. For this reason I am sending to you Timothy, my son whom I love, who is faithful in the Lord. He will remind you of my way of life in Christ Jesus, which agrees with what I teach everywhere in every church.

1 Corinthians 4:15–17

NINE

BEING A FRIEND AND MENTOR

MENTORING IS ONE OF GOD'S PRIMARY
MEANS FOR BRINGING HIS CHILDREN TO
MATURITY. MENTORING WAS A WAY OF LIFE
IN BIBLE TIMES. IT WAS THE PRIMARY MEANS
OF HANDING DOWN SKILLS AND WISDOM
FROM ONE GENERATION TO THE NEXT.

HOWARD HENDRICKS AND
WILLIAMS HENDRICKS

Now we reach one of the most fulfilling, rewarding opportunities for a parent. If we have laid the groundwork for friendship, carefully chosen our words, treated our children as adult friends, let go of them completely, and encouraged them but not rescued them, we may be in the position to become one of our children's life mentors. A mentor is a trusted counselor or guide. In Homer's *Odyssey*, Odysseus left his son, Telemachus, in the care of a guardian named Mentor when Odysseus left to fight in the Trojan War.

The word "mentor" is rich in association. Think about the most significant mentors in your life. Perhaps they were parents, relatives, teachers, pastors, employers, or family friends. How did they impact your life or encourage your faith? Mentoring extends beyond discipling because it focuses on nurturing enduring relationships. While discipling focuses more on the development of one's faith, mentoring can impact all areas of life.

It is critical to understand that becoming a mentor to our adult children is not a decision that we make or a role we request. It hinges on their decision to invite us to share their life journey. A mentor relationship is not imposed or forced on a young person. The young person must seek it out. Just as it is impossible to become adult friends with an intrusive parent, it is equally impossible to cultivate a mentor relationship. Remember from chapter 3 that counsel is like deep water in the well of wisdom (Proverbs 18:4). The discerning person draws up the water (Proverbs 20:5). He or she goes looking for it.

As Iron Sharpens Iron, written by Howard and William Hendricks, is a book about men mentoring one another, based on Proverbs 27:17: "As iron sharpens iron, so one man sharpens the wits of another" (NEB). Beyond the excellent information presented in this volume is the more significant fact that Howard and his son, William, wrote this book together. Their work grew out of deep friendship, respect, and a shared vision. They practiced what they preached.

Howard Hendricks grew up without a father. His parents separated before he was born. He was spiritually mentored by a Sunday school teacher, who led him and several neighborhood boys to Christ by building relationships with them. Hendricks shows us that we don't have to be mentored by our own parents to pass this on to our children.

EARNING THE PRIVILEGE TO MENTOR

> MENTORS DO NOT DIRECT; THEY SHARE WISDOM, LISTEN, AND ENCOURAGE REFLECTION AND ACCOUNTABILITY.
>
> WALTER WRIGHT

Our hope is that our children will seek out our counsel and wisdom when it is needed, desiring us to mentor them. Giving unrequested advice is not mentoring. Keep in mind that we do not want to be our child's sole mentor. The more mentors our children have, the more enriched their lives will be. Our hope is that they will invite us to be *one* of their mentors. Further, we are not looking for a label or waiting for the phone call that begins, "Mom, will you be my mentor?" We understand the shift in our relationships when our children seek us out for wisdom, counsel, support, and guidance. Mentors are trusted and respected. We do not have the automatic right to mentor our children. We must earn the privilege to mentor them.

In Colossians chapter 3, Paul encourages us to "teach each other, and advise each other, in all wisdom" (v. 16 JB). But more important than this instruction are the preceding verses that lay out how we earn the privilege to share wisdom: We are to be compassionate, kind, humble, gentle, patient, forgiving, loving, at peace in Christ, and immersed in His Word (vv. 12–16). Effective mentoring begins with being consistently Christlike.

Mentoring is a relational form of leadership. In selecting leaders for the young church, Paul asked, "If anyone does not know how to manage his own family, how can he take care of God's church? (1 Timothy 3:5). How we relate to our spouses and guide our children is the beginning of our ministry and indicative of our ability to lead and mentor others. Tragically, sometimes churches focus more on the outward behavior of children (and spouses) than on Paul's list of qualities for the leader: self-controlled, gentle, respectable, hospitable, able to teach; *not* violent, quarrelsome, quick-tempered, overbearing, dishonest, greedy, or a drunk (1 Timothy 3:2–5; Titus 1:6–8). The leader described in these verses has invested in healthy relationships and earned the respect of his family. The point for parents is that patterns of being harsh, angry, abrasive, impatient, unforgiving, or arrogant do not lay the groundwork for a mentor relationship.

Significant mentor relationships develop naturally when a young person views an adult engaged in his or her passion (e.g., ministry, music, dance, sports, business), and then asks, "Can you show me how to do that?" Effective teachers know that students become excited about learning when the subject material is relevant to their lives. It is no different when young people observe us following God and ask us to help guide them along their faith journey. Sometimes our adult children may not verbally ask for our counsel, but we observe that they are closely following the example we have set. They seem to know what to do in a challenging situation because they have watched us make solid biblical decisions for years.

WHEN MENTORING CHANGED

> ADULTS TEACH CHILDREN IN THREE IMPORTANT
> WAYS: THE FIRST IS BY EXAMPLE, THE SECOND
> IS BY EXAMPLE, THE THIRD IS BY EXAMPLE.
>
> ALBERT SCHWEITZER

Throughout history, parents and extended family mentored children as they matured. Adult children became apprentices to their older relatives. They were taught a family trade and contributed to their family business. They were spiritually mentored and held accountable by family members. Today we often hear that young people need to grow up in "mentor-rich environments." Until the past century, a young person's life was naturally filled with caring, invested mentors. What changed?

In the industrial age, family-centered communities with generations of extended relatives declined.[1] Families began to trust institutions to educate and guide their children. Teachers and mentors came from outside the family. Then an interesting thing happened. Formal mentoring programs took root as family mentoring relationships weakened. Mentoring became a program, a structured relationship, versus a naturally evolved relationship. "Friendly Visiting" began in the 1880s as a volunteer program. Big

Brothers Big Sisters began as a faith-based organization in the early 1900s and remains one of the strongest mentoring programs today.

In the 1980s an explosion of mentoring programs were founded to help at-risk children and teenagers, and they continue today. Numerous programs in schools and communities match mentors with struggling young people. I know of the following programs in my own community: mentors/advocates for foster children, mentors for children experiencing crisis, mentors for at-risk high school students to help them graduate, writing mentors for inner-city junior high students, and music mentors—world-class musicians who volunteer their time through a local university to teach and mentor at-risk teen musicians, preparing them to enter some of the best music schools in the country. Little Brothers–Friends of the Elderly is a program matching young people with the elderly, as is the Foster Grandparent Program, which benefits both young and old. Do not misunderstand this. Being involved in mentoring programs is an excellent way to reach out and minister to our communities, and Christians should be at the forefront of this work. We should be equally grateful for the mentors in our children's lives. Yet we should not abdicate this role with our own young adult children.

At the other end of the spectrum, we are a society who hires life coaches. We pay for the services of life coaches, career coaches, transition coaches, relational coaches, spiritual coaches, financial coaches, and others to help us navigate our lives. Elka Vera is a life coach who describes her profession as being a personal trainer for the soul. People are hungry for guidance.

In the 1990s some people started to question the effectiveness of mentoring programs for young people. They wondered why the results were not more positive. Those of us who were involved in church discipleship programs in the 1980s and 1990s understand this confusion perfectly. Discipleship became a program instead of arising from a naturally developed relationship. We were assigned to a spiritual mentor or placed in a small group under a leader. The relationships were structured and often artificial. Authentic intimacy and caring cannot be orchestrated or forced. Relationships, not programs, are the core of biblical practice. We invite caring mentors into our lives.

Kristine and Jared became friends with an older couple in their church. As young adults, Kristine and Jared respected Michael and Jennifer. They asked Michael and Jennifer to spiritually mentor them. They began meeting once a week for Bible study and support. Other young couples learned of the meetings and asked if they could join. Soon Michael and Jennifer were mentoring four couples. Their group was not a church-organized Bible study. It naturally evolved out of one young couple drawing up water from the well of wisdom.

> WE HAVE TO DEFINE A MENTOR NOT IN TERMS OF ANY FORMAL ROLE HE CARRIES OUT, BUT IN TERMS OF THE CHARACTER OF HIS RELATIONSHIP WITH THE OTHER PERSON.
>
> HOWARD HENDRICKS AND WILLIAM HENDRICKS

CROSSROADS MENTORING

> EXAMPLE IS THE SCHOOL OF MANKIND, AND THEY WILL LEARN AT NO OTHER.
>
> EDMUND BURKE

Aaron was an exceptional high school student. He was a born leader and excelled in numerous pursuits. He had an impressive background to include on his college applications and was accepted to a fine university. Karen was a hard worker and consistently balanced being a loving mother with expecting the best effort from her son. She provided Aaron with every opportunity to reach for his dreams. A few years later, Karen was surprised to learn that Aaron was not enjoying college and had decided to take a break. She was disappointed that he would not graduate with his class, but she knew that delayed graduation was not unusual. When Karen learned that Aaron had decided not to return to college at all, she cried for a week.

Karen allowed Aaron to move home during his life transition to full-time employment. She charged him monthly rent and set a time limit of three months. As owner and manager of a large company, Karen faced a crossroads decision. As a high school and college student, Aaron had worked in Karen's company during school vacations. She had a position that was perfect for her son, and the company needed his skills as much as he needed employment. She had to decide if offering him a job would be rescuing him or providing an opportunity to professionally mentor him.

Karen had been mentoring Aaron since he was a young boy. When she was driving to visit property sites, five-year-old Aaron would sit in the passenger seat, reading maps and helping her navigate. When everyone else was teaching their children not to talk to strangers, Karen taught young Aaron how to talk to strangers, knowing he would need those skills in business someday. (She was always present to assure his safety.) Since he was a young child, Aaron also watched his mother live out her faith. Karen makes money to give it away, donating to numerous ministries. Aaron learned to take mission trips and help others by observing his mother's generosity.

Karen decided to hire him and continue mentoring her adult son as he apprenticed with her in the business world. He was an excellent employee, soon in charge of multiple projects. When Aaron encountered problems, Karen let him solve them on his own. He lived at home only a few weeks before moving into an apartment.

Aaron respects his mother and says that he has learned more from her than any college business class. Karen believes that she is a better mentor and coach than a buddy or friend. She also taught Aaron to sail in his teen years. As adults, they race sailboats weekly together with other friends. They have established clear lines between their business relationship and their recreational pursuits. Though Karen doesn't view herself first as a friend, Aaron's choice to spend time with her outside of work hours speaks volumes about their relationship. Today Aaron has his own business and his mother is one of his clients.

Biblical Mentoring

> Happy he who has found wisdom, and the man who has acquired understanding; for wisdom is more profitable than silver, and the gain she brings is better than gold.
>
> Proverbs 3:13–14 NEB

The book of Proverbs is about passing the gift of wisdom on to our children. The Lord bestows wisdom, knowledge, understanding, and discernment (Proverbs 2:1–6 JB). Parents are a conduit of these gifts and live them out for their children to see. One theme running through Proverbs is especially relevant today, as evidenced by the downfall of celebrities, politicians, and sports stars due to sexual indiscretions. Proverbs cautions children to follow the godly wisdom of their parents to avoid evil and temptation, specifically sexual temptation. Proverbs repeatedly teaches that adultery will bring ruin (5:1–14; 6:20–26). Following the biblical wisdom of a mentoring parent can avoid this disaster. Proverbs clearly states the antidote for temptation: "Keep your father's principle, my son, do not spurn your mother's teaching. Bind them ever to your heart, tie them around your neck. When you walk, these will guide you, when you lie down, watch over you, when you wake, talk with you" (6:20–22 JB).

When we are not with our adult children, our words and example can continue to guide them, watch over them, and talk to them. We already know that another theme running through Proverbs is carefully choosing our words. The connection may be stronger than we realize. If we practice the ministry of carefully chosen words, nurturing healthy friendships with our adult children, then we may have the opportunity to spiritually mentor them, applying biblical truth to all areas of life, helping them to avoid the minefields. They must first be listening and seeking our input. Our influence grows out of a loving, healthy relationship. Our prayer is that they will remember a lifetime of words in the heat of challenging situations.

It is also clear in Proverbs that we need to listen to our children. My daughter recently said about her peers, "The organized church is answering questions that we are not asking." Observe how radically different this statement is: "The organized church is not answering the questions that we are asking." She thinks the organized church is answering questions that young people are not asking because the church is not taking the time to listen to their hearts and questions. As one well-known expression summarizes, children do not care how much you know until they know how much you care. Effective mentors agree that listening is essential to building relationships. Deadlines and agendas sabotage listening, which often requires sharing generous amounts of unstructured time together.

As described in chapter 2, even Jesus, God incarnate, took the time to first show that He cared. His mentor relationships with His followers naturally evolved. He spent time with them, listened to them, and communicated truth by patiently answering their questions. Jesus did not force His teachings on the disciples; they sought Him out. Jesus earned the right to mentor them.

SHARING WISDOM AND BLESSING

> I WILL GUIDE YOU IN THE PATHS OF WISDOM
> AND LEAD YOU IN HONEST WAYS. AS YOU WALK
> YOU WILL NOT SLIP, AND, IF YOU RUN, NOTHING
> WILL BRING YOU DOWN.
>
> PROVERBS 4:11–12 NEB

In *Courage and Calling*, Gordon Smith states that we have two gifts to share as mentors: wisdom and blessing.[2] Wisdom is a combination of knowledge, experience, perspective, and sound judgment. Wisdom is applied knowledge. Biblical wisdom is the application of scriptural truth in the trenches of life. It is a gift from older people to younger people because older people have probably been through what young adults are experiencing. Blessing is asking for the favor and protection of God. *Blessing* also has additional meanings. My favorite definition is explained by Henri Nouwen in *The Return of the Prodigal Son*: "In Latin, to bless is benedicere, which means literally: saying good things. The Father wants to say, more with his touch than with his voice, good things of his children."[3]

Again we realize that generously sharing encouraging words is critical. Wisdom and blessing are gifts from God to be shared with others, similar to how we share compassion (see 2 Corinthians 1:3–4). We do not hoard wisdom, blessing, comfort, and compassion that we have received from God. We pour it out. John Henry Jowett says, "We must bleed to bless."

THE BOND OF PAUL AND TIMOTHY

> I HOPE IN THE LORD JESUS TO SEND TIMOTHY
> TO YOU SOON, THAT I ALSO MAY BE CHEERED
> WHEN I RECEIVE NEWS ABOUT YOU. I HAVE NO
> ONE ELSE LIKE HIM, WHO TAKES A GENUINE

INTEREST IN YOUR WELFARE. FOR EVERYONE
LOOKS OUT FOR HIS OWN INTERESTS, NOT
THOSE OF JESUS CHRIST. BUT YOU KNOW THAT
TIMOTHY HAS PROVED HIMSELF, BECAUSE AS A
SON WITH HIS FATHER HE HAS SERVED WITH ME
IN THE WORK OF THE GOSPEL.

PHILIPPIANS 2:19–22

Of all the mentor relationships in Scripture, one of the most
intimate is Paul's relationship with Timothy. "I have no one else
like him," writes Paul. Remember that Paul built on the foundation of Timothy's relationship with his mother and grandmother
(2 Timothy 1:5; 3:14). They were his first teachers and mentors.
When Paul invited Timothy to travel with him, Timothy was prepared and ready (Acts 16:1–3).

Paul is an effective mentor to Timothy because he dearly loves
him and often communicates that fact. He calls Timothy his "dear
son" and treats him like a son. He writes in 2 Timothy 1:3–4: "As
night and day I constantly remember you in my prayers. Recalling
your tears, I long to see you, so that I may be filled with joy." Paul
and Timothy have a deep, emotional bond. Timothy is the one
Paul longs to see before he dies. Paul writes, "Do your best to get
here before winter" (2 Timothy 4:21).

Paul gives us a glimpse into his goals for the spiritual children
he mentors. He writes to Timothy: "What you heard from me,
keep as the pattern of sound teaching, with faith and love in Christ
Jesus. Guard the good deposit that was entrusted to you—guard
it with the help of the Holy Spirit who lives in us" (2 Timothy
1:13–14). To the Philippians, Paul writes, "Whatever you have
learned or received or heard from me, or seen in me—put it into
practice. And the God of peace will be with you" (4:9).

This is the tremendous responsibility we have as mentors to
young people, especially our children. Like Paul, we want them

to put into practice what they have learned, received, heard, and seen in us. They cannot model what they have not observed in us. Mentoring begins and ends with good modeling in leading a biblical life. Then we hope that they will guard the good deposit that has been entrusted to them, with the help of the Holy Spirit. In turn, our children can bless and encourage us.

> TIMOTHY BECAME PAUL'S MOST TRUSTED COMPANION AND HELPER. THEIR DIFFERENCES IN AGE RESULTED IN A FATHER-SON RELATIONSHIP, BUT ALWAYS WITH A SENSE OF PARTNERSHIP AND PARITY IN CHRIST. THERE WAS ALSO A REMARKABLE DIFFERENCE IN THEIR TEMPERAMENTS. PAUL COMES ACROSS AS BOLD AND DARING—TIMOTHY, AS SHY AND RESERVED. PAUL WAS EVER THE INNOVATOR AND ADVENTURER. TIMOTHY THE HELPER AND SUPPORTER. IT WAS THEIR EMOTIONAL AND FUNCTIONAL DIFFERENCES THAT CREATED AND NURTURED THEIR CONSTANT NEED FOR EACH OTHER.
>
> GARY DEMAREST

RESCUED MENTORS

> IT'S A BASIC PRINCIPLE OF SPIRITUAL NURTURING: YOU CANNOT IMPART WHAT YOU DO NOT POSSESS.
>
> HOWARD HENDRICKS AND WILLIAM HENDRICKS

Do not assume that one must lead a perfect spiritual life to be a mentor. Sometimes the best mentors have led less than exemplary lives. They have repented and know that they have been rescued by Jesus Christ. When Kenneth was in his early thirties, he had an affair with a coworker that destroyed his first marriage. Today Kenneth is in his fifties and has grown children. He mentors young men in his church who are struggling with sexual temptation, trying to protect them from making the same mistakes he did. They listen to his counsel, just as an alcoholic listens to a recovering alcoholic. Toby was a drug addict in his youth. Since his recovery, he leads a ministry on college campuses to students struggling with drug experimentation and abuse.

In review, effective mentoring is often not the result of a structured program. Nor is it forcing unsolicited advice or an unrequested relationship on young adults, or forcing young adults into the family business. It is not exclusive, but inclusive. Effective mentoring does not begin with a statement ("I have decided to mentor you"), but rather with a question ("Will you mentor me?"). Mentoring offers a biblical example in navigating life, an example that we established long before our wisdom is sought. Later it becomes a response to an invitation to share guidance, counsel, wisdom, blessing, protection, a listening ear, and wise words.

MENTORS DANCE AN INTRICATE TWO-STEP, BECAUSE THEY PRACTICE THE ART OF SUPPORTING AND CHALLENGING MORE OR LESS SIMULTANEOUSLY. GOOD MENTORS HELP TO ANCHOR THE PROMISE OF THE FUTURE. AS YOUNG ADULTS ARE BEGINNING TO THINK CRITICALLY ABOUT SELF AND WORLD, MENTORS GIVE THEM CRUCIAL FORMS OF RECOGNITION, SUPPORT, AND CHALLENGE. THERE IS MORE. MENTORS CARE ABOUT YOUR SOUL.

SHARON DALOZ PARKS

THE IDEAL MENTORING RELATIONSHIP IS PER-HAPS THE "NATURAL" ONE—THE SITUATION WHERE THE MENTOR NATURALLY, ALMOST EFFORTLESSLY OFFERS WHAT HE HAS TO OFFER, AND THE PROTÉGÉ NATURALLY, ALMOST INSTINCTIVELY TAKES WHAT IS OFFERED AND MAKES GOOD USE OF IT . . . MENTORING SHOULD BE A DANCE, NOT A DRILL. ABOVE ALL ELSE, IT SHOULD BRING JOY, NOT GRIEF.

HOWARD HENDRICKS AND WILLIAM HENDRICKS

An adult daughter shares:

My sister and I grew up knowing that we were loved and enjoyed. Dinnertime was the highlight of our day. My parents were playful and silly, but we also had great nightly discussions. My best friend loved to eat dinner at our house. Mealtime was silent at her house. She knew that she was tolerated by her parents, never enjoyed. Our parents always made us feel comfortable sharing anything with them. They told us, "You will never be in trouble if you come to us first and tell us the truth."

My parents were both professional educators. When I was a young student teacher, my assigned mentor teacher was unsupportive and uninvolved, leaving me to flounder. I wanted to quit but my parents encouraged me to persevere. They became my mentors and passed their teaching knowledge and experience on to me. After I had been teaching for several years, I was frequently absent during one semester due to illness and surgeries. My students were struggling, enduring rotating substitutes. My mom, a retired teacher, became my long-term substitute. She used an alias so my students did not know that she was my mother.

When friends comment that I remind them of my mother, I accept this as the highest compliment. My parents are now deceased but when I am teaching, I feel that I am carrying on their legacy.

It may be surprising to learn that my parents separated (never divorced) after my sister and I left home to attend college. Yet they even handled that well. Though they became too incompatible to live together after we buffers were gone, they remained close friends and kept our family intact. We celebrated all holidays, birthdays, and special events together. If I was performing in a concert, my parents would attend together. Sometimes when my sister and I were busy, our parents would go out to share meals and conversation on their own. I have used their example to encourage my students' families who face divorce.

My sister and I always remained the mutual priority in our parents' lives, and our friendship with our parents only became stronger as we reached adulthood. They modeled this relationship for us, despite their differences.

An adult daughter shares:

My mom and I are close friends. Even when we disagree, we can be honest with each other and are always there for one another. My mom has also been an exceptional mentor, both a spiritual as well as a career mentor. I am a professional writer and editor who works for the Jerry B. Jenkins Christian Writers Guild. My younger sister is now training to be a professional writer. Mom began our careers by reading to us every day when we were young and sharing the wonderful world of story. Later, Mom included us in her editing process on her books and asked for our opinions about her work. She taught by example. I observed that she lived out her faith in her work.

Mom always encouraged us by saying, "Good job. Next time try this . . ." instead of saying, "Don't do this or that. That's wrong." She helped us to start publishing as high school students. When I entered a college writing program, she took some of the classes with me. Today our roles have shifted. I have become a mentor to her. She sends me her work to review and edit. I share my resources and contacts with her. I include her in my professional world, just as she did for me as I was growing up.

A mother shares:

When I was a young adult, my dad mentored me in our family business and I later mentored my adult son and daughter in the same business. I view this experience through the eyes of a daughter as well as a mother. I learned from my dad what to do and what not to do as a mentor.

My dad's business consumed his life. As much as my dad loves me and would do anything for me, he couldn't develop a good relationship with me outside of work. We've always depended on each other when we needed help but we haven't enjoyed a friendship. I have worked hard to become friends with my adult children. I wanted to mentor my children spiritually and try to mirror Jesus Christ to them, inside and outside of the workplace.

I was a director in my dad's business and learned important skills that I've passed on to my children. The most important gift I received from my dad was a can-do spirit. He believed there is a solution to every problem if we set our minds to figure it out. I have observed my children adopt this mind-set in their own careers.

As grateful as I am for the business skills my dad taught me, I need to share the whole story. I received a college music scholarship after I graduated from high school. I would have loved to become a teacher of music and other subjects. My dad discouraged me from pursuing college. He wanted me to remain in our town and work in his business. I respected his wishes and turned down the opportunity. In hindsight, I wish that my dad could have encouraged me to pursue my own dreams.

In mentoring my adult children, I've offered them business training but never forced it on them. I've encouraged them to pursue their own passions. My daughter is now married with a son. We hang out together and enjoy each other's company. My adult children often come over for dinner. My son brings friends to our home who don't have good relationships with their families. Our children come to my husband and me when they need help or advice. Sometimes they just need to talk. Sometimes they do not follow our advice. We respect their decisions. We are careful to not give them unrequested advice. We are honest that we don't have all the answers in life. Our job is to encourage and support our children in whatever they do.

A father's a treasure; a brother's a comfort; a friend is both.

Benjamin Franklin

In all the hurry to make a difference, many mentors can forget to take time to build a relationship, to give credence and weight to the process of establishing a firm connection. This means carefully building trust. The cardinal rule of mentoring is to listen to youth, a practice that seems to define effective mentors more than any other.

Marc Freedman

If instead of a gem, or even a flower, we should cast the gift of a loving thought into the heart of a friend, that would be giving as the angels give.

George MacDonald

TEN

EXPANDING OUR CIRCLE
OF FRIENDSHIP

GIVING MORE THAN RECEIVING IS THE BEST
WAY TO WORK ON THE SOUL.

THOMAS MOORE

We have different roles in our relationships through various seasons of life. Sometimes we plant the seed in someone's life and other times we water the seed, but only God makes the seed grow (1 Corinthians 3:6–8). Just as other adults water the seed we have planted in our children's lives, we can water and fertilize the seeds planted by other parents.

Hara Marano observes an alarming pattern in society where helicopter parents are so focused on their own children's well-being and success that they have no interest in investing in other children.[1] Hopefully followers of Jesus Christ stand in sharp contrast, as the care we lovingly provide for our children extends to other young people, like ripples in a pond. Even Paul, who focused on mentoring others, mentions Rufus's mother as being like a mother to him (Romans 16:13).

We can befriend and mentor our children's peer friends. We can mentor and minister to young people in our churches and communities. We have the privilege of loving and embracing our children's spouses as if they were our own children. We can share generous doses of wisdom and blessing with our grandchildren. Radiating out from how we nurture friendship with our immediate family, we recognize limitless opportunities to befriend, encourage, influence, and mentor the people that God places in our lives.

Embracing Our Parents and Relatives

> Here's a truth about postparenting. If you haven't come to love, forgive, and accept your own parents, it's very tough for your children to do so with you.
>
> Jane Adams

Whether we experience easy or difficult relationships with our own parents or in-laws, we realize that our children are learning about adult friendship from watching us. They learn how to treat us as we age by observing how we treat our parents and extended family.

Joan and her mother had always been best friends. Now that her mom has dementia, she becomes furious with Joan and berates her when she visits. Joan tries to be compassionate, remembering the years when her mother spoke kind words to her. Corrine's mother was an alcoholic. Like many adults who grew up in neglectful or abusive families, Corrine broke the chain to raise her children in a loving, stable, Christ-centered home. She learned from observing her mother what not to do as a mother and grandmother. Corrine did her best to maintain a friendship with her mother, caring for her until she died.

Every Christmas, Debbie gives her mother-in-law the gift of spending one afternoon a week together, helping her with anything she desires. Kris told me that her mother-in-law was more than a second mom; she became one of her closest friends as Kris nursed her mother-in-law in her own home until her death.

Donna made a choice as a newlywed to become friends with her husband's mother. Donna called her by her first name, Kate. No matter what her mother-in-law said or did, Donna chose to not be offended. Through the years, Donna became closer to Kate than her own mother. Donna and her husband brought Kate to live with them in her final years. Donna believes that we can extend friendship backward and forward through the generations. It depends on us.

DECIDING TO REACH OUT AND EMBRACE

> NOW THAT YOU HAVE PURIFIED YOURSELVES BY OBEYING THE TRUTH SO THAT YOU HAVE SINCERE LOVE FOR YOUR BROTHERS, LOVE ONE ANOTHER DEEPLY, FROM THE HEART.
>
> 1 PETER 1:22

When we befriend and mentor the people in our lives, we provide a model for our children. They will pass this on when they follow our example and reach out to others. We can mentor our children's peer friends through opening our homes to them and making them feel that they are part of our families. Melanie takes two of her dance students (also her daughter's close friends) out for coffee monthly. These students live with challenges at home, and Melanie offers time for them to talk and share their struggles. She drives them to church activities with her daughter. Melanie also provides their dance classes at a discounted tuition.

Paul makes an effort to spend time with his daughters' serious boyfriends so that the groundwork will be laid if their relationships develop into engagement and marriage. Paul told me, "I don't want the first serious conversation I have with my future sons-in-law to be when they ask for my blessing to marry my daughters. I want to start building friendships as early as possible so that they will feel comfortable coming to talk to me about anything. Of course, I've developed good relationships with young men who never became fiancés, but I hope they are better men because of it. Young people can never have too many adults who care about them."

Not all relationships begin as ideal friendships. A decision is consciously made to extend friendship. Several parents have told me, "I would not have chosen that person to be my child's spouse but once they married, I decided to love him/her and welcome him/her into our family." These parents decide to view their family as expanding to include a new son or daughter instead of losing a child. They embrace, not compete with, their child's in-laws. Remembering how much her parents hated their respective in-laws, Donna wrote her new daughter-in-law a letter, welcoming her into the family and giving her freedom. She clearly stated, "I want to be your friend. You don't have to call me Mom unless you want to. You don't have to clean your house when I come over because then I will feel the need to clean my house when you visit me. You don't have to spend every holiday with our family. I know that you have a family too."

The better friends we are with our children, the more opportunities we will have to spend time with and influence our grandchildren. Jacquie and Tim have raised three adult children. Their eldest son, Ryan, and his wife, Faith, live near them and attend their church. Jacquie and Tim care for their grandchild one day a week while Ryan and Faith are working. Faith's parents care for their grandchild on other days. All the grandparents make a good team.

Jacquie and Tim's second son, Kyle, attended college across the country and then moved to England to pursue his career. Kyle met a widow with two young children. They married and remained in England. Kyle adopted his wife's children and loves them like his own. Because they were so young when their father died, these children will only know Kyle as their father.

Jacquie and Tim made a decision to embrace Kyle's wife and love her children as their own grandchildren. They make regular trips to England to visit Kyle and his family. Kyle's wife has told Jacquie how grateful she is for her son. Kyle is the answer to all her prayers.

Other grandparents coordinate with parents to take their grandchildren on individual, special vacations. One couple host "Cousin Camp" in their home for a week every summer, enjoying their grandchildren, creating bonds and memories between cousins, and giving their adult children a needed break and time alone with their spouses.

Janice married a man with four young adult children, who were not excited about having a new stepmother. She decided to love and mentor them, calling herself their "bonus mom." She earned their trust and now has the privilege of being an active grandma in their young children's lives. Janice also has invested her time in mentoring the children of her close friends. She is "Aunt Janice" and doesn't miss one special event to celebrate her numerous adopted nieces and nephews. She is also passionate about reaching out to orphans and annually travels to Africa to work with a ministry that builds orphanages for children with AIDS.

During the Christmas season, Janice plans a big party for her own son and her stepchildren's families the week before Christmas to avoid conflicts with her stepchildren's biological mother and in-law family celebrations. Every child and grandchild receives a giant stocking stuffed with fun gifts. This past year, Janice's son visited his girlfriend's family for Christmas weekend while her stepchildren were busy with their respective families. Janice could have moped around because she and her husband were spending Christmas alone, wondering where their Christmas invitation was. Instead Janice invited all of her friends and adopted nieces and nephews who were not spending Christmas with relatives to Christmas Eve dinner. On Christmas Day, Janice went to a church to serve Christmas dinner to the homeless. No matter the logistical challenges she encounters, Janice makes it a practice to reach out to family, friends, and strangers in need. "Poor me" is a phrase not found in her vocabulary. She tells me, "I have so much to be grateful for. I want to share it with others."

Kent and Marnie were unable to have children of their own so they became godparents and "aunt and uncle" to their closest friends' children. They decided to become active mentors to these young people, walking beside their friends in raising their children. Scott, a pastor, and Christy, a teacher, did not have their own children so they opened their home to foster children. Now that their foster children are legal adults, Scott and Christy continue to be involved in guiding their lives. Since Scott grew up with a harsh, critical father, he understands how much young people need unconditional love and acceptance. Childless as a young woman, Sarah decided to open her home to foster children. Now eighty-five-year-old Sarah receives cards and gifts on Mother's Day from her 150 former foster children.

Since Kathryn was once a foster child, she has dedicated her adult life to mentoring foster children who turned eighteen without a home base or family support. She helps them apply to college, secure financial assistance, and find employment. Jason mentors at-risk teenagers in a continuation high school, helping them to stay on track to graduate. Because Janet gave birth to a baby when she was sixteen years old, she volunteers her time at a continuation high school for teen moms, helping them plan for their future. Antonio spent time in prison as a young man before having his life transformed by Jesus Christ. Today he mentors male teens in juvenile hall, offering them hope in changing their life direction.

IT IS NEVER TOO LATE

Perhaps while you were reading this book, you wished that you had a healthier relationship with your children. You may see an opportunity to nurture a closer relationship with your parents, siblings, in-laws, or other relatives. Perhaps you enjoy a good friendship with your children but now see the possibilities for befriending and mentoring your nieces, nephews, stepchildren,

children's spouses, grandchildren, friends' children, and other young people. No matter your different relationships, the message to remember is: *It is never too late.* You can build better friendships with the people God has placed in your life, no matter where you start.

THEN THE RIGHTEOUS WILL ANSWER HIM, "LORD, WHEN DID WE SEE YOU HUNGRY AND FEED YOU, OR THIRSTY AND GIVE YOU SOMETHING TO DRINK? WHEN DID WE SEE YOU A STRANGER AND INVITE YOU IN, OR NEEDING CLOTHES AND CLOTHE YOU? WHEN DID WE SEE YOU SICK OR IN PRISON AND GO TO VISIT YOU?" THE KING WILL REPLY, "I TELL YOU THE TRUTH, WHATEVER YOU DID FOR ONE OF THE LEAST OF THESE BROTHERS OF MINE, YOU DID FOR ME."

MATTHEW 25:37–40

IN EVERYTHING I DID, I SHOWED YOU THAT BY THIS KIND OF HARD WORK WE MUST HELP THE WEAK, REMEMBERING THE WORDS THE LORD JESUS HIMSELF SAID: "IT IS MORE BLESSED TO GIVE THAN TO RECEIVE."

ACTS 20:35

An adult son shares:

My dad died in an accident when I was a young teenager. My dad's friends reached out to me. One friend tutored me in math, another took me on fishing trips, and one friend, Mike, came to help my mom and me with a variety of tasks. Two years later Mike and my mom married. He loved her, took care of her, and made her very happy. He also became a wonderful dad to me. Because Mike was quite different from my own dad, he taught me new skills and gave me new insights. He didn't try to replace my dad. I have been blessed with two great dads in my life and am a better man for it. Now that I have my own family, Mike has been an equally wonderful grandfather to my children.

An adult daughter shares:

When I was a teenager and struggling to communicate with my parents, my aunt was a great sounding board. She made the effort to spend time with me. Sometimes we went out for coffee or to see a movie. She was always available to talk on the phone if I needed her. She held the same biblical views that my parents did but didn't judge or criticize me. She could listen to me. Since she didn't take my rebellion personally, she never reacted in anger and I could share my frustrations in a safe place. In hindsight, I realize that she was mentoring and guiding me when I wasn't comfortable talking to my parents.

An adult son shares:

I grew up in a Christian home where my parents were always helping people in need. We fed hungry people. We housed aging relatives as well as struggling people who had no place to go. We helped drug addicts start new lives. We offered a safe place for abuse victims to recover. My parents lived out Christ's commands. They walked their talk. Now when I see someone in trouble, I offer my assistance. I just can't help it.

An adult daughter shares:

We are never too old to enjoy a mutual friendship with our parents. As a middle-aged woman, I realized one day that when my husband, adult children, and friends are all busy, my ninety-four-year-old mother always has time for me. For a lifetime, she has made time for me. She still cooks for me when I visit. She constantly prays for her grandchildren and is passionately interested in their lives. Since they support themselves, she is a generous giver on their birthdays and holidays, easing their financial pressures. My mother has always been a remarkable role model but watching her age gracefully with dignity has been her most important life lesson yet. When I asked her once how I could repay her for everything she had done for me, she replied, "Don't give it back. Pass it on to your children." I honor her by trying to follow her example.

I have urged you to never be a quitter, to never give up, to stay at the task even when the outlook is bleak. Now I want to clarify that this means you are on your own. I have not abandoned you, but I have cut you loose. And just as it is important for me to let you go and make your own mistakes, so it is vital that you not see me or our home as a way station that would keep you from building your own muscle. My door is shut so you'll know I believe you can solve your own problems, find your own solutions, develop your own strategies. I am, of course, still your friend, so if and when I can help you as a friend would, I am here. And when you need an ear, I'm here. When you need a loan—not a gift—if I am able, I'm here. And, even though that door is shut, it will always be unlocked for you. You see, the day may come when life defeats you. If you are injured or ill to the point that you can't function, I am still your parent; we are still your family. If you fail so miserably that your options are gone and you can't go on, by all means know that here, with us, you have a refuge. You may be so bitterly disappointed or grieving that you simply need to know that someone is behind you. Never doubt it. If you lose a spouse, a child, or a home, you are still part of this family. You may have left and cleaved to someone else, but you still have a refuge.

Jerry B. Jenkins, *As You Leave Home: Parting Thoughts from a Loving Parent*

OUR TREASURED PRIVILEGE

LORD, REMIND ME OFTEN THAT PARENTS
ARE INTENDED TO BE A MOORING POST, A
SAFE PLACE TO STAY, A SURE PLACE TO CAST
ANCHOR COME WIND OR WEATHER.

JILL BRISCOE

During a business dinner that I was attending with my husband, guests were sharing about their children. One woman said, "I have two children and I wish that I had never had them." I can only imagine the deep heartache behind that honest statement. Enjoyable friendships do not naturally develop between parents and children.

My son had an unusual view of this book. I formally interviewed my grown daughters just as I interviewed many young adults. They had important insights that I have included in these pages. They both said, "You are going to interview our brother, aren't you?" I knew I should interview my son, but I wasn't sure he would be receptive. I braved asking for his insights, which were short, not sweet. I could have predicted his first response, "That's a silly topic." My analytical son (mathematician/engineer) explained, "You can't be friends with your parents. We choose our friends. We can't choose our parents, hence we cannot become friends. It's an entirely different type of close relationship."

My eldest daughter observes that it is the parents' job to naturally ease into friendships with adult children. My other daughter

believes that it is as much the child's job as the parent's job to
nurture an adult friendship. And my son thinks that friendship
between parents and children is not a realistic pursuit. You are
probably familiar with Eustache Deschamps's famous quote,
which we warmly embrace as we adopt friends into our families: "Friends are relatives you make for yourself." My son said the
opposite: Relatives cannot be friends you make for yourself. Yet
my son feels close to his family. I've learned that we are his anchor
as he adventures into the world. He teases his sisters for calling
home every time they need to talk, counting on our emotional
cheerleading and support. My son is a reserved, capable young
man, who knows we are here if he needs us. Loving him from afar
continually reminds me of my husband's favorite quote, "Ships are
safe in the harbor but that's not what ships are for."

After reading this book, your views may be as varied as my
own children's. There is no formula for nurturing healthy, intimate family relationships. Your adult friendships with each of your
children will be as unique as they are.

In closing, let's review what we now understand about nurturing friendships with our adult children.

We sow the seeds for friendship in childhood. We invest in
a long process of relationship building, hoping to earn the trust,
respect, love, and friendship of our children. Becoming adult
friends does not happen overnight nor is it automatic.

We can confidently rely on Jesus Christ as our model for
parenting. Using wise words, carefully listening to our children,
and treating them as adult friends are the critical keys to healthy
friendship.

We have been stewards of our children and realize that they
belong to God. We ferociously protected them when they were
young and now we completely let go to get out of God's way as
He guides them and raises them to maturity. We aim to find the
balance between offering the emotional security of a safety net yet
not rescuing them. We know that we can remain friends and keep

communication lines open when we disagree with our children's choices. Offering the unconditional love and forgiveness of Jesus Christ is different than offering approval.

It is our privilege to encourage our children through life's challenges and mentor them along the journey, if we are invited. Our lifetime example of following God undergirds their path.

As an outgrowth of our friendship, we can embrace our children's spouses and new families, and reach out to other people, young and old. We celebrate that our family grows and expands, and is always inclusive.

Enjoying a close friendship with the child we birthed and raised is a precious treasure of unsurpassed worth that deserves to be treated with the utmost loving care. We may have many close friends throughout life, yet enjoying an intimate lifetime friendship with our own children is the privilege we prize.

> IF A TRUE FRIENDSHIP CAN BE FOUND, CHERISH IT LIKE A FINE GEM. POLISH IT, GO OUT OF YOUR WAY TO KEEP AND PROTECT IT. KEEP IT SAFE, BUT LET IT SHINE FOR ITSELF. IT WILL GROW AND GROW.
>
> MARY SWANEY

Notes

Introduction: A Garland of Grace

1. Donald Miller, *Searching for God Knows What* (Nashville: Thomas Nelson, 2004), 113.

Chapter 1: Sounding the Alarm

1. Hara Estroff Marano, *A Nation of Wimps: The High Cost of Invasive Parenting* (New York: Broadway Books, 2008), 176.

2. Ibid., 213.

3. Ibid., 126.

4. Diane Worthey, "Butterfly Dust," *American Suzuki Journal* (Winter 2009): 19.

5. Marano, *Nation of Wimps*, 19.

6. Ibid., 20.

7. Ibid., 179.

Chapter 3: Laying the Foundation for Friendship

1. Susan Lieberman, *New Traditions: Redefining Celebrations for Today's Family* (New York: Noonday Press, 1991), 10.

2. Maurice J. Elias, Brian S. Friedlander, and Steven E. Tobias, *Emotionally Intelligent Parenting* (New York: Harmony Books, 1999), 39.

Chapter 4: Using Our Words Wisely

1. C. Hassell Bullock, *An Introduction to the Old Testament Poetic Books* (Chicago: Moody Press, 1979), 160.

Chapter 6: Letting Go Completely

1. Gordon Smith, *Courage and Calling* (Downers Grove, IL: InterVarsity Press, 1999), 109.

2. Richard Beaton and Linda Wagener, "Flourishing 101," *Fuller Theology, News, & Notes* (Spring 2010): 7.

CHAPTER 7: BEING A FRIEND WHEN WE DON'T AGREE WITH OUR CHILDREN'S CHOICES

1. Philip Yancey, *What's So Amazing about Grace?* (Grand Rapids: Zondervan, 1997), 137.

2. For a more in-depth look at forgiveness, see chapters 13–14 of my book *Living with Thorns: A Biblical Survival Guide* (Grand Rapids: Discovery House, 2009).

CHAPTER 8: BEING A FRIEND AND ENCOURAGER

1. Stormie Omartian, *The Power of Praying for Your Adult Children* (Eugene, OR: Harvest House, 2009), 9.

2. Mary Ann Froehlich and PeggySue Wells, *What to Do When You Don't Know What to Say* (Minneapolis: Bethany House, 2000), 63.

CHAPTER 9: BEING A FRIEND AND MENTOR

1. The technological revolution has only accelerated this disconnection.

2. Gordon Smith, *Courage and Calling* (Downers Grove, IL: InterVarsity Press, 1999), 70.

3. Henri Nouwen, *The Return of the Prodigal Son* (New York: Doubleday, 1992), 96.

CHAPTER 10: EXPANDING OUR CIRCLE OF FRIENDSHIP

1. Hara Estroff Marano, *A Nation of Wimps: The High Cost of Invasive Parenting* (New York: Broadway Books, 2008), 229.

NOTE TO THE READER

The publisher invites you to share your response to the message of this book by writing Discovery House Publishers, P.O. Box 3566, Grand Rapids, MI 49501, U.S.A. For information about other Discovery House books, music, videos, or DVDs, contact us at the same address or call 1-800-653-8333. Find us on the Internet at http://www.dhp.org/ or send e-mail to books@dhp.org.

ABOUT THE AUTHOR

Mary Ann Froehlich is a board-certified music therapist and Suzuki music teacher. She and her husband, John, have three adult children. Mary Ann has worked in hospitals, schools, churches, and private practice. She has published articles, music, and twelve books, including *Living with Thorns: A Biblical Survival Guide*, *An Early Journey Home: Helping Families Work through the Loss of a Child*, and *Facing the Empty Nest: Avoiding a Midlife Meltdown When Your Child Leaves Home*.

Mary Ann has a doctorate in music from the University of Southern California and an MA from Fuller Theological Seminary.